Performance Measurement, Reporting, Obstacles and Accountability

Recent Trends and Future Directions

Performance Measurement, Reporting, Obstacles and Accountability

Recent Trends and Future Directions

Paul G. Thomas
Duff Roblin Professor of Government
Department of Political Studies
University of Manitoba

ANU

THE AUSTRALIAN NATIONAL UNIVERSITY

E PRESS

ANU

E PRESS

the Australia and New Zealand
School of Government

Published by ANU E Press
The Australian National University
Canberra ACT 0200, Australia
Email: anuepress@anu.edu.au
Web: http://epress.anu.edu.au

National Library of Australia
Cataloguing-in-Publication entry

Thomas, Paul, 1943- .
Performance measurement, reporting, obstacles and
accountability : recent trends and future directions.

Bibliography
ISBN 1 920942 78 5 (pbk.)
ISBN 1 920942 79 3 (online)

1. Personnel management. 2. Performance standards. 3.
Performance - Measurement. I. Title.

658.3125

This monograph is based upon material previously published in Optimum On-Line
(http://www.optimumonline.ca/) and by the Saskatchewan Institute for Public Policy
(http://www.uregina.ca/sipp/). The author gratefully acknowledges their support for
this publication.

Cover design by John Butcher

Funding for this monograph series has been provided by the Australia and New
Zealand School of Government Research Program.

John Wanna, *Series Editor*

Professor John Wanna is the Sir John Bunting Chair of Public Administration at the Research School of Social Sciences at The Australian National University. He is the director of research for the Australian and New Zealand School of Government (ANZSOG). He is also a joint appointment with the Department of Politics and Public Policy at Griffith University and a principal researcher with two research centres: the Governance and Public Policy Research Centre and the nationally-funded Key Centre in Ethics, Law, Justice and Governance at Griffith University. Professor Wanna has produced around 17 books including two national text books on policy and public management. He has produced a number of research-based studies on budgeting and financial management including: *Budgetary Management and Control* (1990); *Managing Public Expenditure* (2000), *From Accounting to Accountability* (2001) and, most recently, *Controlling Public Expenditure* (2003). He has just completed a study of state level leadership covering all the state and territory leaders — entitled *Yes Premier: Labor leadership in Australia's states and territories* — and has edited a book on Westminster Legacies in Asia and the Pacific — *Westminster Legacies: Democracy and responsible government in Asia and the Pacific*. He was a chief investigator in a major Australian Research Council funded study of the Future of Governance in Australia (1999-2001) involving Griffith and the ANU. His research interests include Australian and comparative politics, public expenditure and budgeting, and government-business relations. He also writes on Australian politics in newspapers such as *The Australian*, *Courier-Mail* and *Canberra Times* and has been a regular state political commentator on ABC radio and TV.

Table of Contents

Foreword

Paul G. Thomas has taken a major interest in the issue of performance measurement and management and has written extensively on the subject. The following monograph first appeared as two articles:

- 'Performance Measurement, Reporting and Accountability: Recent Trends and Future Directions', *Saskatchewan Institute of Public Policy Paper No 23* February 2004; (http://www.uregina.ca/sipp/) and
- 'Performance Management and Management in the Public Sector', *Optimum Online — The Journal of Public Sector Management* Vol 35, Issue 2, July 2005. (http://www.optimumonline.ca/)

They are re-presented here in a single, wide-ranging and provocative monograph that offers much to the academic researcher, the policy practitioner and those at the 'coal face' who sometimes struggle to implement appropriate measures of what they do.

Together, these works traverse the area of performance measurement as practiced by governments in Canada, the US, Australia and New Zealand and consider, not only why performance management is useful and necessary, but also the difficulties inherent in it.

Professor Thomas debunks the myth that 'if you can't measure it, you can't manage it' and shows how the resources required to 'do' performance management can sometimes exceed the expected gains. Lastly, governments need to think about actually using the results they achieve from performance management and of tailoring their performance measurement activities to their needs and their resources.

I am sure that this very practical material will be very useful to managers in the Australian and New Zealand contexts as it provides both an overview of what has been done overseas and also a sensible appraisal of the range of available tools and approaches.

Readers who wish to explore in more depth are provided with an extensive bibliography of sources with recommendations for further reading.

John Wanna
Sir John Bunting Chair of Public Administration
ANZSOG
Research School of Social Sciences
The Australian National University
Canberra ACT 0200

About the Author

Paul G. Thomas is a Professor in the Department of Political Studies, University of Manitoba, where he has taught since 1969. He holds a BA (Hon) and MA degree from the University of Manitoba and a Ph.D. from the University of Toronto. He is the co-author of the best-selling textbook *Canadian Public Administration*. (Prentice Hall, 1987). He is the author of more than 50 journal articles and book chapters on topics such as parliamentary reform, party caucuses, budgeting, crown corporations, regulation, constitutional reform, organisational change in the public sector, ministerial responsibility and accountability, contracting out the delivery of public services, and performance measurement in the public sector.

He has been a consultant on numerous occasions to federal and provincial governments and to several royal commission and task forces. He served as the first Academic Director of the Manitoba Legislative Internship from 1985 to 1988. In 1985-1986, he was a member of the City of Winnipeg Act Review Committee. From 1987 to 1989 he served as the Chairperson of the Board of Directors of the Manitoba Telephone System. From 1993 to 1999 he served as Editor of the journal, *Canadian Public Administration*, published by the Institute of Public Administration of Canada. In October 1994, Professor Thomas received the Lieutenant Governor's Medal for Excellence in Public Administration awarded by the Institute of Public Administration (Manitoba Chapter) and from 1996 to 2002 he was a Senior Fellow of the Canadian Centre for Management Development in Ottawa.

He has twice won university-wide teaching awards and the Outreach Award for the University of Manitoba. In December 1999, he was named the first Duff Roblin Professor of Government at the University of Manitoba. During 2000–2001 he chaired a Review and Implementation Committee, which provided advice to the Minister of Health on the recommendations of the *Paediatric Cardiac Surgery Inquest Report*. He served during 2001 as a member of the Advisory Committee to the task force reviewing the Access to Information Act at the federal level. During 2001–2003, he was the Chairperson of the Regional Planning Advisory Committee, which is preparing recommendations to the Government of Manitoba for a regional plan for Manitoba's Capital Region.

In 2003, Professor Thomas was awarded by the Institute of Public Administration of Canada the Vanier Medal for exceptional achievement in public administration. Since 2004, he has chaired the Board of Directors of the Manitoba Institute for Patient Safety, and from 2005 he has served on the Board of Directors of the Canadian Patient Safety Institute.

Introduction

The Government is extremely fond of amassing great quantities of statistics. These are raised to the nth degree, the cube roots are extracted and the results are arranged into elaborate and impressive displays. What must be kept in mind, however, is that in every case, the figures are first put down by a village watchman and he puts down anything he damn well pleases.

Sir Josiah Stamp, Her Majesty's Collector of Inland Revenues, more than a century ago.

As the quotation from Sir Josiah Stamp suggests, governments have long collected information about their own performance and about their impacts on society. A healthy scepticism has always surrounded such data. However, in recent years performance measurement and performance reporting have become even more important within most governments. 'If you can't measure it, you can't manage it' has become a familiar refrain.

Performance measurement and a number of related processes are seen as the key tools of performance management within public organisations. There is a confusing array of buzzwords used on this general topic: reinventing government, new public management, performance management, results-driven government, results-based budgeting, performance contracting, etc. Whatever the name of the initiative and the actual techniques, the common goal is to improve the performance of government and to enhance its value to society. For the purpose of this paper, performance measurement will be defined as the regular generation, collection, analysis, reporting and utilisation of a range of data related to the operation of public organisations and public programs, including data on inputs, outputs and outcomes.

The theory behind these approaches seems simple and straightforward. On the other hand, the actual experience with performance reporting and performance management is, at best, mixed. It is easier to find examples of where performance measurement systems have been abandoned or drastically scaled back than it is to find examples where such systems have become an influential feature of government decision-making and have contributed demonstrably to improved performance by public organisations. Therefore, this paper asks the question: 'What makes performance measurement so attractive in theory, yet so difficult in practice?' There is not an easy, single and non-controversial answer to this seemingly simple question. Different analysts would emphasise different factors in explaining why performance measurement systems have generally been disappointing in terms of the actual use of performance data to guide decision-making and to achieve improved performance.

There are a great many things done by government that cannot be measured. Given the problems of attribution, all measures of program impacts must remain open to debate as to their validity, reliability and significance. Furthermore, there is no technical procedure available to rank and to combine different types of measures to reach a judgement about the relative worth of different policies and programs. Such judgements must ultimately be left to the political process. The real value of performance measurement and reporting comes not from providing the 'right' answers, but by helping to frame questions and to structure a dialogue about how to improve public services.

Performance measurement and performance management will remain important approaches to the improvement of government performance and to the restoration of citizen confidence about government spending. However, after four decades of design and development of measurement systems, the emphasis must now shift to how we use measurement to manage better. Utilisation has been the Achilles heel of performance measurement and performance reporting. The discouraging record of non-use of performance information has many causes. As performance measurement systems enter a more mature phase, the challenge for governments is to ensure that measurement influences actions, which in turn deliver results. The greatest obstacles to the integration of measurement and management are human and cultural, not analytical and technical. Developing a culture of performance management will require sustained, shared leadership and a more systematic approach to cultural change than has been followed to date.

Some commentators emphasise the analytical challenges involved in applying the concepts of performance measurement to public policies and public programs. Developing measures to track **inputs** (the combination of money, staff, materials and other resources) and **outputs** (the goals, services and activities produced) is fairly straightforward and governments have made significant progress on this front. However, we have a long way to go in terms of providing valid and reliable measures of **outcomes** (the actual impacts of policies and programs within society). The development of causal models which allow us to attribute outcomes to programs and to distinguish program impacts from non-program effects within society continues to be difficult in most program fields. The analytical challenges to valid measurement become even greater when we attempt to measure the overall success of policy in such broad fields like health, social policy, the environment, where complex interactions take place among different jurisdictions, their programs and the activities of other actors within society.

Other commentators would emphasise the institutional obstacles to successful performance measurement in the public sector. They would argue that it is simply naïve and unrealistic to expect public organisations and the people who work in them to conduct and to present unbiased and complete accounts of their own performance. Also, the nature of public sector goals (multiple, vague, shifting and even conflicting), the structure of the public sector (hierarchical, rigid and fragmented) and the written and unwritten rules of behaviour (compliance with red tape, an insistence on no mistakes, the avoidance of blame, etc.), all represent additional institutional obstacles to the adoption and use of performance measurement systems.

Another explanation might be financial. The development of comprehensive and reliable performance measurement systems is expensive, both in terms of generating data, staff time and investments in information technology. In the last several decades, however, money and staff have been in short supply. Governments have launched performance measurement systems at the same time they have been downsizing their public services and cutting budgets. Indeed, many public servants fear that performance measurement is nothing more than a budgetary axe intended to cut down a perceived jungle of overgrown programs and organisations. If performance measurement is directly and immediately linked to resource allocation decisions, it becomes more of a potential threat to programs and bureaucracies and there is a greater incentive for public managers to report selectively on performance.

While these analytical, institutional and financial obstacles are obviously part of the explanation for the disappointing record of performance measurement, this paper offers more of a political explanation. In this perspective, performance measurement is viewed as a subjective, value-laden activity, taking place in a political context. Performance measurement systems are not strictly objective and neutral in their operation and their effects. They have an impact on the distribution of authority and influence within organisations, as well as on the types of evidence deemed legitimate to guide decision-making. For the staunchest advocates, the development of performance information is meant to reduce the extent of decision-making based upon narrow, self-interested calculations, whether these calculations are made by politicians, bureaucrats or both.

However, performance measurement can never — and should never — be completely divorced from 'politics' in the broadest sense of that term. By politics I mean the process for recognising and accommodating competing values, interests and demands to define the public interest. Performance measurement can contribute to this process, but we must recognise its limits. Also, if we want performance information to improve the 'quality' of political debate and public sector decision-making, then we will have to design performance measurement systems to serve the needs of elected politicians. Many proponents of performance measurement recognise the political context in which they are working. However, the content and the reporting of performance results often do not encourage utilisation by politicians because they fail to directly address their most immediate and compelling concerns.

This monograph identifies the ways that 'politics' enters into the creation of performance measurement systems, the selection of the official and unofficial aims of such systems, the selection of performance criteria and measures, the interpretation of findings, the responses to such findings and the implications of performance reporting for the accountability of both politicians and public servants. Along the way, both the conditions favouring and the obstacles to successful performance measurement will be highlighted.

The Origins of Performance Measurement

Many trends and conditions inside and outside of government have driven the current widespread interest in the use of performance measurement to improve the performance of government in general and the individual organisations which comprise it. These factors are discussed at length elsewhere and therefore need only be briefly listed here:

- the stressed financial condition of most governments with accumulated debts and annual deficits, which are only now being brought under control;
- the turbulent and unpredictable environment of today's public sector which requires governments to have both a sense of direction and the capacity to respond expeditiously to unforeseen changes, creating a need to track trends and developments more carefully than in the past;
- the impact of new public management philosophies, which are leading, rhetorically at least, to an insistence on results rather than an adherence to prescribed procedures, to the removal of excessive central agency controls over line departments, the delegation of more authority to public managers;
- the transfer of program and service responsibilities to other orders of governments (usually at the provincial/state or local level) and to the private for-profit or non-profit sectors of society;
- the need to respond to several decades of slow, but steady decline of public trust and confidence in governments by strengthening accountability and improving communication with respect to public programs;
- the need to respond to the growing public insistence that service quality in the public sector must improve; and
- the opportunity to take advantage of the refinements in analytical techniques and new information technologies, which enable more sophisticated tracking of the success of programs and offer opportunities to improve the democratic dialogue over public policy. [1]

The spread of performance measurement reflects and reinforces these trends. From the perspective of this paper, it is important to note that both external, 'political' forces as well as internal, 'managerial' considerations lie behind the recent popularity of performance measurement. This means there is the risk that what began as a managerial tool in the private sector, namely performance measurement, will be mistaken for a solution to essentially political problems that have arisen from the fundamental changes taking place outside and within public sector organisations.

Another way to analyse the emergence of performance measurement is to think of the existence in the contemporary public sector of four types of deficits. During the 1980s and the 1990s, most of the talk, and nearly all the actions of governments, were intended to deal with the 'financial' deficit. However, by the end of those decades, there was a growing recognition of the existence of three other types of deficits. First, there was a 'social deficit', consisting of the unmet needs arising from the cumulative impact of two decades of budgetary restraint and cutbacks. Second, there was a 'performance' deficit consisting of the gap which the public perceived between what they were paying for government in terms of taxes and the value of the programs and services they were receiving, which seemed to be less than in the past. Thirdly, there was the so-called 'democratic deficit' which refers to the declining legitimacy and public confidence in political institutions, such as elections, political parties, legislatures, governments and public services. Empirical studies suggest that the sources of public discontent with the political system are many, including both short-term and long-term factors.[2] This means that a single institutional reform or set of reforms is not likely to completely resolve the problem. Adoption of performance measurement and performance reporting has often been oversold as a solution to all four types of deficits — financial, social, performance and democratic. Realism requires a recognition that its contribution is likely to be limited, especially to the co-called democratic deficit.

In summary, performance measurement achieved popularity in response to the difficult changing conditions of the public sector at the end of the 20th century. However, the concept was not brand new. It had been part of the 'grab bag' of private management techniques — such as planning, programming budgeting, management by objectives and total quality management — applied to the public sector, with generally disappointing results, during earlier decades. Back then performance measurement was being used to guide the expansion of the public sector in an era when money was more available and public services were growing, and public confidence in the capacity of governments to achieve progress was relatively high. Today resource scarcity, downsizing of public services and public scepticism towards the role of government are the prevailing conditions. This makes performance measurement a potentially threatening activity for both the producers and the beneficiaries of public programs. Faced with the stresses described above, beleaguered public sector leaders, whether elected or appointed, have been under intense pressure to improve the performance and the reputations of the organisations they lead.

ENDNOTES

[1] See Arie Halachmi and Geert Bouckaert (eds.). *Organisational Performance and Measurement in the Public Sector*. Westport, Ct. Quorum Books, (1996) and John Mayne and Eduardo Zapico-Goni (eds.). *Monitoring Performance in the Public Sector: Future Directions from International Experience*. New Brunswick, N.J. Transaction, 1997.

[2] See the discussion and the sources found in Paul G. Thomas, 'The Impact of Information Technology and the Future of Representative Democracy' in Maurice Demers (ed.). *Governance in the 21st Century.* Ottawa: Canadian Centre for Management Development, 2001.

The Lexicon of Performance

Wherever there is government, there is government performance. On the basis of such obvious statements, modest reputations are earned! However, what constitutes performance within government is more complicated, pluralistic, value laden, and controversial than is true with the performance of private firms where the meaning and the yardsticks to measure successful performance are more limited and more universally accepted. In government, performance is usually thought of as progress toward goals and objectives, but measurement is complicated by the fact that the outcomes being sought are often multiple, vague, shifting, and even conflicting; this reflects the fact that they emerge out of the wider political process of competitive political parties and public debate. In diverse countries such as Canada or Australia, individuals, groups, and regions will often disagree strongly over what constitutes good performance. Also, government performance is more subject than corporate performance to continuous, usually critical, scrutiny by opposition parties, interest groups and the media. So, for governments, appearances matter almost as much or more than the reality of performance. For public managers who operate programs, part of the performance equation is no surprises and keeping the ministers they serve out of political trouble. Maintaining legitimacy and support for the policies and programs of government is also a legitimate performance goal. In short, performance is a many splendoured thing, and good performance is partly in the eye of the beholder.

From the vantage point of today's world, where most governments talk the language of performance and have invested heavily in the development of measurement systems, it is instructive to recognise that until quite recently the practice of measuring performance in order to strengthen it was relatively uncharted territory. Writing in the early 1970s, Alice Rivlin, a highly respected policy analyst, endorsed the value of this approach in words that today sound self-evident:

> It therefore seems to me that analysts who want to help improve social service delivery should give high priority to developing and refining measures of performance. Relatively little effort has gone into devising such measures so far, despite their importance and the apparent intellectual challenge of the task. Performance measures for social services are not, of course, ends in themselves. They are prerequisites to attempts both to find more effective methods of delivering social services and to construct incentives that will encourage their use. (*Systematic Thinking for Social Action*, 1973)

Recognising the intellectual challenge of the task, Rivlin cautioned against confusing different components of performance, especially effort and achievement, with one another. This warning remains relevant because when we talk about performance, we may mean inputs, outputs (efforts), or outcomes (achievements, whether immediate or long-term) within society. These three dimensions of performance are causally linked, but not always in ways that are well understood. Moreover, performance measurement can focus on any or all of these dimensions. A common practice, particularly in the early days of performance measurement but still used now, is to equate measuring effort with measuring achievement.

A comprehensive definition of performance measurement would include the regular generation, collection, analysis and reporting of a range of data related to the operation and the impact of public organisations and public programs. Performance measurement emerged as a major activity within governments during the 1980s and 1990s in response to such familiar trends and developments as mounting deficits and debt, the impact of new public management philosophies, the use of contracting out and public/private partnerships to deliver programs and services, the growing public insistence that service quality and results must improve, and the need to respond to several decades of slow, but steady decline of public confidence in governments by strengthening accountability and improving communications about performance. The availability of refinements in analytical techniques and of new information technologies both drove and assisted the move toward performance measurement.

Measuring and reporting on performance is a necessary but not sufficient requirement for improving performance and for assuring the public that they are receiving value for money from public programs and public organisations. A related, but somewhat different activity, 'performance management', is meant to build upon measurement by using performance information in conjunction with strategic planning, budgeting, policy/program evaluations, organisational reviews, and performance appraisals for managers. In this way, performance measurement potentially becomes central to the processes of direction setting, control, quality assurance, accountability, improvement and learning within the public sector. Integrating measurement and management represents the biggest challenge for the future.

The Aims of Performance Measurement

Given their diverse origins, it is not surprising that multiple aims have been attached to the recently launched performance measurement systems. Often the aims are stated in highly positive terms. For example, the Kennedy School of Government at Harvard University begins its case for the use of performance measurement with the following statement: 'Effective performance management leads to better outcomes and strengthens democracy.'[1] As **Exhibit 1** indicates, the aims of performance measurement range from the narrowly managerial to the broadly political. Different purposes will require different types of measures. There is not one single magical measure or set of measures that will serve all these purposes equally well.[2] For example, if the principal aim is to achieve budgetary control and productivity, the focus will be on efficiency measures such as the costs of providing a certain volume of output on an annual basis. In contrast, if the aim is to promote public understanding and support for a program, it will be necessary to gather evidence of dimensions of performance about which people really care. Since performance measurement systems are costly to create and to maintain, there are practical limits on the number of dimensions of performance that can be measured on an ongoing basis. Also, the proliferation of measures can lead to information overload.

Exhibit 1 — The Aims of Performance Measurement

- To help clarify organisation goals, directions and expectation.
- To help organisations learn how to accomplish goals more effectively.
- To communicate the priorities of the organisation.
- To support strategic/business line planning by linking broad statements of direction to specific operational outputs and outcomes.
- To support budgetary planning and resource allocation processes.
- To monitor the operation of programs and to make continuous improvements.
- To motivate public servants and to restore pride within the public service that it is making a positive contribution.
- To enable citizens to make better informed decisions in the use of public programs.
- To restore public confidence that they are receiving value for money in public spending.
- To assess whether the organisation is achieving its goals.
- To strengthen internal administrative and external political accountability.

Multiple aims means multiple potential audiences for performance information and multiple, subjective perspectives on what constitutes good performance.[3] Citizens will naturally think about performance mainly in personal terms — often based on how they perceived their most recent encounter with government or their general impressions of how governments work. Elected politicians often talk about using performance measurement to track general improvement in economic, social and environmental conditions. They are also deeply interested in how policies and programs affect various 'constituencies', not just of the territorial variety, but also economic and social in character. Performance measurement systems that fail to address distributional questions (who benefits and who pays) may not speak to these considerations.

For a number of reasons, governing has become a more adversarial process than in the past. In cabinet-parliamentary systems, of course, it is the job of the opposition parties to criticise the government. The aggressive partisanship and the negative theatrics featured prominently in legislatures largely prevent constructive debates about performance matters. Ministers will seek to avoid the publicity and controversy that 'bad news' brings — reacting defensively when something goes wrong. For their part, opposition parties can usually be counted on to interpret mistakes and shortcomings in performance in the worst possible light. When such clashes take place and are reported in the media, the issues involved become amplified and distorted. The whole process contributes to the public's impression that nothing or little in government works as intended.

Public servants are interested in performance, but they also recognise the informal rules of the current accountability and rewards systems which operate in government. Ministers want error free government. When mistakes or just unforeseen and unwanted events occur, public servants are expected to provide a rationalisation to minimise the damage to the reputation of the minister and the government. With increasing frequency individual public servants are named and blamed for untoward events, even if the problems in question arise from flaws in policy or resource limits which are ultimately controlled by ministers. More is said on the problems separating political from administrative accountability for performance later in this article.

In summary, performance measurement has been asked to serve numerous purposes, which are both 'political' and 'administrative' in character. Not all of these aims are consistent and it is impossible for any single performance measurement system to serve them all equally well.

Different users approach the issue of performance differently. The aims, focus, methods and uses of performance measurement reflect both political and bureaucratic considerations. Performance reports have the potential to set the agenda both inside government and in the external world of public debate. Poor reports can damage ministerial reputations and negatively affect the position and resources of departments and programs. In short, there are risks involved with the collection and the publication of performance information. These realities of the practice of performance measurement can be contrasted with the image of a rational and objective process presented in the official reports.

ENDNOTES

[1] Harvard University, Kennedy School of Government, Executive Session on Performance Management, 2001 (Downloaded from www.ksg.harvard.edu/visions/performance-management).

[2] Robert D. Behn. "Different Purposes Require Different Measures" (Paper presented to the Association for Public Policy Analysis and Management. Seattle, November 2-4, 2000).

[3] Robert D. Behn. "The Psychological Barriers to Performance Management: Or Why Isn't Everyone Jumping on the Performance Management Bandwagon." *Public Performance and Management Review* 26, 1 (September 2002). pp. 5-25.

The Ideal of Performance Measurement

Implicit in the government reports and the secondary literature promoting performance measurement is an image of an 'ideal' system. The key features of this ideal system are as follows. (See **Exhibit 2**.) It gives most attention to impacts or outcomes, not just to descriptions of activities and to volumes of outputs. It employs a focused, manageable and cost-effective set of measures. The measures are valid, clear, consistent, comparable, and controllable, in the sense that they measure matters over which the organisation has control. The measures must also be relevant, meaningful and informative to the leaders/funders of the organisation. Evidence from the system must be presented in a balanced, comprehensive, and understandable and credible fashion. The performance measurement system is embedded in the organisation, it is linked to other key activities like planning and budgeting, it is a source of intelligence which guides decision-making on a regular basis and it is an institutionalised part of the culture of the organisation to which people throughout the organisation are committed. This image of the ideal performance measurement system represents an aspirational statement rather than a description of what is. Most systems fall far short of the ideal, which may represent a destination that is never reached because of the problematic and controversial nature of the whole enterprise. There needs to be more realism in the discussions of the potential and the problems of applying the performance measurement approach to the public sector.

Exhibit 2 — The 'Ideal' Performance Measurement System — A Destination Never Reached

- It has clearly defined purposes and uses.
- It focuses on outcomes, not just on inputs and outputs.
- It employs a limited, cost effective set of measures.
- It uses measures which are valid, reliable, consistent, comparable and controllable.
- It produces information which is relevant, meaningful, balanced and valued by the leaders/funders of the organisation.
- It is integrated with the planning and budgetary processes.
- It is embedded in the organisation, is stable and is widely understood and supported.

In somewhat less abstract terms, the Canadian Comprehensive Auditing Foundation (CCAF) has developed nine principles 'to provide direction for future advances in performance reporting in Canada.'[1] **Exhibit 3** presents the nine principles. According to the CCAF, the principles 'reflect a unique integration of the differing perspectives of legislators, managers and auditors — three groups with an important stake in public performance reporting.'[2] The first five principles provide guidance about **what** governments should report, while the remaining four relate to **how** governments report. The principles 'start out as ideals, the ceiling that reporting aspires to reach', but over time they become 'standards, the floor below which reporting may not sink.'[3] Taken as a set, the nine principles are meant to provide a framework for performance reporting. The CCAF recognises that there are obstacles to applying the principles, that different governments and individual organisations within them will have greater or less difficulty in applying the principles, and that organisations will be at varying stages of readiness to apply the principles.

Exhibit 3 — Nine Principles of Better Performance Reporting

1. Focus on the few critical aspects of performance.
2. Look forward as well as back.
3. Explain key risk considerations.
4. Explain key capacity considerations.
5. Explain other factors critical to performance.
6. Integrate financial and non-financial information.
7. Provide comparative information.
8. Present credible information, fairly interpreted.
9. Disclose the basis for reporting.

Canadian Comprehensive Auditing Foundation, Reporting Principles: Taking Public Performance Reporting to a New Level. Ottawa, 2002.

There is much that is sensible and realistic in the CCAF's principles and the discussion of their implementation. Because the CCAF report focuses on performance reporting, a great deal of attention is paid to the communications requirements for building a sound performance measurement system. There is a recognition of the need for leadership and communication to gain understanding, acceptance and legitimacy for the system with employees of the organisation, and with other stakeholders. There is a recognition of the need to tell the 'performance story' and not become too mesmerised by the numbers themselves. Developing a strategic communications approach to performance reporting is discussed later in this paper. Suffice to say at this point, that formal performance reporting is only one window through which internal and external audiences will gain information and form impressions about performance. To call for more and better reporting assumes that the relevant audiences will read the documents and use them to judge performance. There is evidence to be discussed later, which suggests this optimistic assumption does not apply for all audiences at all times.

ENDNOTES

[1] Canadian Comprehensive Auditing foundation. *Reporting Principles: Taking Public Performance Reporting to a New Level.* Ottawa: CCAF-FCVI inc. 2002. p.3.

[2] *Ibid.* p. 3.

[3] *Ibid.* p. 17.

Defining Performance

Given the multiple aims and multiple potential users of performance evidence, controversy can arise from the outset over how to define 'performance'. Much of the literature implies that performance is an objective phenomenon, consisting of a set of attributes of a program and its measurable impacts on society. It is as if 'performance' was 'out there', just waiting to be discovered and documented through a set of measures or indicators. In reality, however, performance is a social construct. The interpretations and the measures of performance arises as much, if not more, out of an interactive process among individuals and institutions, as they do out of theories of programs, data generation and analysis. As Rob Paton writes, 'Performance is what those people centrally involved in and concerned about an organisation agree, implicitly and explicitly, to be performance.'[1] Defining performance in this way, of course, detracts from the claim that performance measurement systems provide objective, reliable and scientifically valid evidence about what works and what doesn't in the public sector.

Performance will always remain a contested and evolving concept. Securing agreement on what constitutes performance, especially successful performance, is made more difficult by the nature of public sector activity. Most public programs have more than one goal and the goal statements tend to be vague, changeable, controversial and, at times, conflicting. Under these conditions, performance is a multi-faceted and subjective phenomenon. There are usually numerous stakeholders — that is, individuals and organisations who can affect or are affected by public programs — and therefore there can be widely divergent perspectives on what constitutes performance. Unlike private firms for which profits and returns on investment provide widely accepted measures of success, for public organisations the criteria of success are many and controversial.

There is also a significant symbolic component to the actions of government, consisting of the language and images used to describe what is taking place and the public's reactions to those messages.[2] Appearances matter almost as much as reality. The adoption of a performance measurement system, often accompanied by considerable fanfare, is itself meant to send the reassuring message that in the future government decision-making will be based more on objective evidence about longer-term impacts than on short-term political calculations. The implication is that we can get 'the politics' out of program management, allowing design and delivery of programs to be based upon well-informed professional judgements. There is also a 'performance art' aspect to performance measurement. Doing performance measurement can become a ritualistic activity intended to satisfy or impress significant others — such as Treasury Boards, or funding agencies if outside organisations are involved.

In summary, the performance captured by a particular set of measures will always be partial and contextual, reflecting the fact that the measures have been selected, analysed and interpreted through the lenses of the organisations and individuals involved with the process. This is quite different from the claim that performance measurement systems can provide objective evidence about how well an organisation or program is operating. Given their inherently subjective nature, all measures should remain open to debate and possible replacement. When particular measures cease to be debatable, there are three possible explanations:

- the measures do not focus on significant dimensions of performance;
- or, a particular conception of the organisation's goals and how to achieve them has gained dominance to the extent that debate has been stifled; and
- or, the activity of performance measurement has become a routinised, ritualistic part of organisational life which is not taken seriously.

Regardless of which of these conditions apply, the result will be to impair organisational learning and improved performance. An acceptance of ambiguity, contingency, plurality, and controversy can be seen as signs of organisational health, not as signs of confusion, lack of clarity and poor performance. Finding an appropriate balance between confidence and commitment to a particular set of measures versus ongoing debate and revisions to the measures, is an important part of the art of performance measurement.

Two simplistic slogans appear frequently in the performance management literature. The first is that 'you can't manage what you can't measure.' If this were in fact true, the largest and most important parts of organisational life would not be subject to managerial direction and control. It is the 'softer', more submerged dimensions of organisational life which have been shown to be crucial to better performance. The second slogan exhorts leaders within organisations to 'manage by the numbers'. Exactly how this is to be done is not made clear, nor are the dangers of doing so identified. Setting performance targets and basing decisions on performance results may cause organisations to do the wrong things well if they become too committed to a particular understanding of policy problems.

ENDNOTES

[1] Rob Paton. *Managing and Measuring Social Enterprises*. London: Sage, 2003. p. 5.

[2] See Murray Edelman. *Political Language: Words That Succeed, Policies That Fail*. New York: Academic Press, 1977.

Comparing Approaches to Performance Measurement

Performance measurement has become so widespread that it is impossible to know all that is taking place within governments across the world.[1] Also, the labels and the focus of performance measurement systems shift, usually when a new government takes office. Positive, action-oriented words are usually chosen as names for such systems — 'Measuring Up' in Alberta, the 'Oregon Benchmarks', the 'Minnesota Milestones' and 'Best Value' in the United Kingdom. Despite such inspirational language, some of the early leading performance measurement systems have recently been reduced in scope or dropped entirely. Keeping track of the rise and fall of performance measurement systems is made somewhat easier by the Internet (government websites, on-line reports and electronic journals) but the problem has become information overload and knowing what credibility should be assigned to the 'official' descriptions, given that governments are interested in promoting the best possible reputation for their efforts.

There is no single, 'one best' approach to performance measurement. A government needs to develop an approach that fits with its constitutional/institutional arrangements, its political and administrative traditions, its size and organisational capabilities, its current environment and issues and, not least important, what it can afford. The tendency has been for governments to apply a single approach uniformly to all departments, non-departmental bodies and programs. This 'across-the-board' approach may have the apparent virtues of consistency, comparability and fairness, but it is not without problems. The fundamental problem is that organisations and programs differ in the extent to which they are amenable to measurement, especially in terms of linking outcomes in society to programs. Routine, operational programs with narrower goals and better understood production processes allow for easier and more coherent measurement than 'softer' programs serving broader, more controversial goals, the achievement of which is not well understood and/or depends upon the exercise of a wide measure of professional discretion and judgement. In view of these differences, there is the legitimate concern that the use of performance measurement, especially an insistence on quantification of outcomes and benefits, will create an institutionalised bias in favour of so-called 'hard' programs whose production processes are relatively well understood. The need for balance between quantification and relying on the numbers versus qualitative evidence and telling the 'performance story' is examined later in this paper.

During the past decade, the federal and provincial governments in Canada have developed two broad approaches to the development of measures and indicators of performance. In Alberta, Nova Scotia, Ontario and Quebec, governments have reported on the performance of the entire government in terms of the presumed impacts of their activities on society. This 'social-indicator' type of approach supports external, political accountability by providing information which relates to the concerns of citizens. However, the selection of indicators to feature in 'report cards' to citizens is inherently arbitrary (why waiting lists for surgeries rather than impacts of preventative measures in health care?), and the problems of attributing changing economic and social conditions to government actions or inactions is next to impossible. Other provinces and the Government of Canada began their performance measurement efforts by requiring individual departments to prepare business plans and performance reports. The 'business-line' approach is more of a managerial tool than something which would normally be used by politicians and the public.

These two broad approaches — the system-wide and the business-line — could be pursued simultaneously and complement one another. This has been the evolution of the performance reporting system in the Government of Canada. It began by publishing performance reports on a departmental basis and now more than 80 such documents for departmental and non-departmental bodies are tabled in Parliament on a annual basis. Beginning in 2001, the President of the Treasury Board also released on an annual basis a report to Canadians covering nineteen social indicators, reflecting the four themes of economic opportunities, health, the environment and the strength and safety of Canadian communities.[2]

This evolution can be contrasted with Manitoba's experience. Under the Progressive Conservative government of Premier Gary Filmon (1988–1999), the province adopted a program called 'Manitoba Measures' based upon the departmental business plans model. Conferences, training sessions and investments in performance measurement took place as departments began to create the capacity demanded by the 'centre' of government. Then, after the New Democratic Party (NDP) took office in September, 1999, the 'Manitoba Measures' program was abruptly dropped. A full post-mortem of its demise has yet to be written, but it seems the new government believed that the program was ineffective because it did not address the real concerns of politicians and was not integrated with program planning and budgeting. Presumably encouraged by the new government, the Manitoba Bureau of Statistics began development of a 'Manitoba Well Being Index' which would track economic, social and environmental conditions to produce an aggregate measure of 'total well being'. Just as the 'business line' approach seemed to be consistent with the 'market' philosophy of the Progressive Conservatives, the 'social well being' approach matched the NDP's commitment to a broader role for government.

Even when governments limit their performance measurement efforts to individual departments and programs, the problems of defining and measuring successful performance is only slightly less challenging. Governments have developed a number of different frameworks to identify successful programs. Probably the most common framework involves the so-called 'three big Es': economy, efficiency and effectiveness. In simple terms each of the three Es can be described as follows:

Economy	-	Have resources been acquired at least cost?
Efficiency	-	Are the inputs (people, money, supplies) being combined to produce the maximum volume of outputs (goods and services)?
Effectiveness	-	Are the goals of the organisation/program being met, without undue unintended consequences?

These elements have been at the centre of all the 'rational' management approaches applied to the public sector over the past four or five decades. However, the framework does not cover some dimensions of performance. It does not cover the fourth Big E, equity, which deals with the distributional impacts of performance. Omitting equity may have an impact on another important E in government, namely electability. In recent years, many governments have added a 'customer satisfaction' component to the effectiveness component of the three E model. Also, the framework does not directly address the issue of the capability and desirability of delivering a designated set of results.

In its earlier program evaluation scheme, the Government of Canada indicated that a program was deemed to be well performing when it was:

Relevant	-	Continues to be consistent with government-wide and department priorities
Successful	-	Continues to be consistent with government-wide and department priorities
Cost-effective	-	Involves the most appropriate and efficient means to achieve goals.

This framework deals with the desirability of continuing a program, but not the issue of whether the organisation has the capability and capacity to deliver the desired results.

Organisational report cards represent another type of performance measurement and reporting.

Exhibit 4 presents one interpretation of the requirements for such report cards. In 1987 the Canadian Comprehensive Audit Foundation (CCAF) published a report on 'organisational effectiveness' which incorporated a broad definition of performance. The attributes of an effective organisation were:

- management direction
- relevance
- appropriateness
- achievement of purpose
- acceptance
- secondary impacts
- costs and productivity
- responsiveness
- financial results
- working environment
- monitoring and reporting

Several jurisdictions have since applied this framework, including for crown corporations in the federal government and hospitals in some provinces. The framework incorporates features of previous approaches and does address more directly the issue of future organisational capacity to deliver results. Operational meanings behind indicators have to be assigned to each of the attributes. There may be conflict in practice among the attributes — e.g., cost efficiency may reduce responsiveness. Finally, the issue of aggregating data on each dimension to arrive at some overall judgement about effectiveness is a challenge.

Exhibit 4 — Organisational Report Cards — Criteria for Design

- Validity
- Comprehensiveness
- Comprehensibility
- Relevance
- Reasonableness
- Functionality

William T. Gormley and David L. Weimer, *Organisational Report Cards*. Cambridge, Mass.: Harvard University Press, 1999. pp. 36-7

The final framework to be discussed here comes out of the management audit work of the Office of the Auditor General of Canada (OAG). The OAG distinguishes among six different components of performance:

1. Mission statements
2. Results statements
3. Performance indicators/measures
4. Performance expectations/targets/commitments
5. Strategies/activities

6.   Performance accomplishments/achievements

As befits the role of a legislative auditor, this framework emphasises the desirability of integrating performance planning, budgeting, monitoring and reporting. The framework also stresses external accountability for results. These two topics are addressed later in this paper.

ENDNOTES

[1] The journal *Public Performance and Management Review* is a rich source of comparative information, as is the OECD's Public Management Service. (Available at http://www.oecd.org/puma).

[2] President of the Treasury Board, Canada's Performance 2002, Annual Report to Parliament. Ottawa: Treasury board Secretariat, 2002.

Choosing Measures/Indicators

Regardless of the approach adopted, a sound performance measurement system must have three qualities: it must be technically valid, it must be functional, and it must be legitimate. For a system to be legitimate in the eyes of those who operate programs or are directly affected by them, it is usually necessary to involve such institutions and individuals in the development of the measures. Stakeholder agreement on measures will not only improve the measures themselves, as it will also help to overcome potential resistance and to increase the prospects for actual utilisation. There is general agreement on the desirable technical attributes of a set of measures. **Exhibit 5** presents one generic listing of the 'ideal' qualities of such a system. What is functional for a particular organisation is best left to the judgement of the leadership of that organisation.

Most government manuals on performance measurement make a distinction between performance measures and performance indicators. Ideally, performance measures report unambiguously on the relationships that exist between program activities and the outputs and outcomes associated with them. However, as various writers have pointed out, most relationships between programs and societal impacts are imperfectly understood and subject to change over time. For example, if we are to understand the relationship between safety regulation in the transportation field and the reduction of fatalities and injuries, we must control the impact of other influences within the program environment. Despite refinements in our analytical tools over the past several decades, the technical challenges involved with the production of valid performance measures for the most important and costly public programs remain formidable performance indicators are said to be less precise than actual measures of program impacts. They usually provide only a proxy indication of the performance of a program or policy system. Whereas measures might be likened to numbers on a gauge, performance indicators might be compared to alarm bells. Like the bell on the cat in the famous fable, performance indicators tied to particular programs or to broader policy systems can warn when unpleasant surprises are on the way, as well as inform managers of program success. Given the current state of our knowledge about many programs, the distinction between true measures and approximate indicators is somewhat artificial, since most measures in use by governments today have their limits, are open to interpretation, and, therefore, should be the subject of debate rather than of automatic acceptance.

Exhibit 5 - Ideal Performance Indicators

Clarity. Performance indices should be simple, well defined, and easily understood.

Consistency. The definitions used to produce the indicators should be consistent over time and between units.

Comparability. Following from consistency, it is only reasonable to compare like with like.

Controllability. The manager's performance should only be measured for those areas over which he or she has control.

Contingency. Performance is not independent of the environment within which decisions are made. The environment also includes the organisation structure, the management style adopted, as well as the uncertainty and complexity of the external environment.

Comprehensive. Do the indicators reflect those aspects of behaviour that are important to management decision-makers?

Bounded. Concentrate on a limited number of key indices of performance — those most likely to give the biggest pay-off.

Relevance. Many applications require specific performance indicators that are relevant to their special needs and conditions. Do the indicators service these needs?

Feasibility. Are the targets based on unrealistic expectations? Can the targets be reached through reasonable actions?

Peter M. Jackson, *Measures for Success in the Public Sector.*

There is strong push within the performance measurement movement to have organisations produce comparative evidence on performance. The comparisons can be to other comparable organisations within a sector or within the same organisation over time. 'Benchmarking' and the adoption of the 'best practices' of leading organisations is part of this trend. It is assumed that gathering and reporting comparative information creates a powerful incentive for improvement and learning from others. Less recognised are the risks involved, particularly from assuming that what appears to work in other organisations can be readily and easily transferred to a organisation in a different context. Rob Paton, in his careful study of the performance measurement efforts of non profits in the United Kingdom, concludes that 'efforts to pin down performance and to identify the sources of success through measurement achieve only limited success'.[1] He found that most organisations employed the language of best practice, but rarely followed all of the operational steps involved with the approach. The aspirational component of the approach — striving to do better — helped to sustain managerial attention to important issues and some important ideas were imported to organisations through comparisons.

From my perspective, it would be wiser for organisations to pursue a 'smart practice' rather than a 'best practice' approach. Smart practice recognises that in statistical terms all organisations cannot be 'the best'. Under the benchmarking approach, choosing the best organisation for comparison purposes is both crucial and problematic. Organisations deemed to be the best at one point in time by one set of measures often lose that status in the near future. Exhorting organisations to strive for 'the best in class' status may ignore the practical limits faced by a given organisation, such as lack of leadership talent and support, inadequate resources, limited and inappropriately qualified personnel, an organisational culture which is unsupportive, etc. When the rhetorical elements are swept away and 'the best practice' consultants are shown the door, most public managers would continue to 'network' and to draw from the experiences of others. This is the essence of benchmarking and best practice without the veneer of scientific certainty. Developing reliable and consistent information for comparison purposes is a worthy goal, but it has to be balanced by the harm such information can cause, by the costs involved and by the potential of such information to provide the basis for improvement.

ENDNOTES

[1] Paton, *op. cit.* p. 43.

Linking Performance Measurement to Planning

As mentioned above, many jurisdictions now insist that performance measurement be directly linked to strategic planning and/or 'business line' planning. Ideally, strategic planning helps organisations to clarify their mission, mandate and goals, to scan the future external and internal environments for threats and opportunities, to identify strategic issues and alternative ways to deal with them, and to develop a set of outcome indicators to track progress towards their goals. All of these elements are to be linked to annual operational planning and to forthcoming budgets. This might be called the 'textbook model' of strategic planning. It represents the aspiration to achieve predictable, comprehensive, systematic and rational control over the future direction of the organisation in all dimensions of its performance.

Perhaps the leading example of an attempt to link comprehensive planning to performance measurement is the Government Performance and Results Act (GPRA) passed by the Congress of the United States in 1993. The Office of Management and Budget within the executive branch was a key champion of this initiative. But the fact that Congress made planning and performance measurement a statutory requirement reflected the independence of the legislative branch from the executive within a political system based on the constitutional principles of the separation of powers and checks and balances. This is fundamentally different from the cabinet — parliamentary systems in Canada where authority is concentrated in the hands of the Prime Minister and the Cabinet and, in principle the permanent bureaucracy owes an undivided loyalty to the government of the day.

The adoption of the GPRA is seen as an important marker in the history of administrative reform in the United States. Not surprisingly with such a major event, there are contradictory assessments of what the Act has accomplished.[1] In terms of the basic requirements of the Act, they were as follows:

- all agencies (with a small number of exceptions) were required to submit five-year strategic plans, which include annual performance plans with measurable goals and performance targets;
- plans were to be updated very three years;
- annual performance reports were to be submitted to Congress starting in 2000; and,
- by 2002 agency performance reports were to show three-year comparative data for indicators of program performance.

The GPRA made it clear that the performance plans and performance reports were to be concise and comprehensible. They were to be the main source of internal accountability within departments and of external accountability to Congress.

How has the GPRA worked in practice over the past ten years? The record is mixed, but most informed commentators conclude that overall it has been disappointing. A recent article (2003) pointed to the following kinds of implementation problems:

- the OMB found that in 20 percent of the performance plans it reviewed, the measures were not precise enough to use in management and budgeting;
- 76 percent of program managers reported that their programs, projects or operations had measures, but these measures were not results oriented;
- reliance upon third parties (e.g. states and non-profits) to deliver programs made it difficult to obtain accurate and comparable data; and,
- agency results were affected by outside events and isolating program from non-program impacts was exceedingly difficult.

When the General Accounting Office (the audit and evaluation agency which supports Congress) reviewed performance plans and reports in 1997, no agency received better than a C grade and the majority received Fs.[2]

There are technical, institutional and financial causes of this disappointing record, but Professor Nancy Roberts offers a more fundamental explanation. She writes: "The synoptic model of strategic planning that the GPRA champions is a poor fit for many bureaus to the extent that they confront value and stakeholder conflicts, manage crosscutting programs and experience a high degree of change and instability in their task and general environments."[3] Her comments reflect an ongoing debate in the management literature over whether comprehensive planning is even possible in government. Sceptics insist that in practice, planning in the public sector resembles strategic improvisation or what Robert Behn calls 'management by groping along' (MBGA).

MBGA combines a general sense of direction with an experimental, trial-and-error approach to discovering what works. Using the MBGA approach, reflective public managers recognise earlier rather than later that a particular initiative has gone off course. It is also argued that the 'one-size-fits-all' approach to strategic planning does not recognise the differences among public sector organisations in terms of the relative precision of their mandates, the complexity of their production processes and the stability of their external and internal environments. This means that organisations will differ in the extent to which they are able to follow formal planning models as opposed to a more informal strategic improvisation approach. The latter approach is more intuitive and therefore makes less use of formal analysis, including performance indicators, but it may be more 'rational' because it matches the conditions of decision-making in the real world.

ENDNOTES

[1] See the article by Nancy Roberts. 'The Synoptic Model of Strategic Planning and the GPRA'. *Public Productivity and Management Review* 23, 3 (March 2000). pp. 297-311 for a list of commentaries, including reports from the General Accounting Office which serves Congress.

[2] Roberts, *op. cit.* p. 298.

[3] Roberts, *op. cit.* p. 309.

Integrating Budgeting and Performance Measurement

All of the advocates of performance measurement favour incorporating performance-based information into the formulation of budgets. The real issue is how this is to be done and the extent to which performance information should drive budgetary decision-making. It is more than a coincidence that performance measurement initiatives in most governments have been launched and controlled by central budgetary agencies (whether these are called Treasury Boards, Management Boards or other titles) and by the funding authorities for outside third parties engaged in the delivery of public services. However, the relative merits of a centralised unilateral, uniform, forced and strictly regimented approach versus a decentralised, consultative, flexible, gradual and more experimental approach, are still being debated.

'Performance-based budgeting' has become a popular, but poorly defined term. In a general sense, it might be thought of as the practice of determining the budget of a program or a department on the basis of its past or anticipated future levels of performance. More precisely, according to John Mercer, a key architect of the GPRA in the US, 'real performance-based budgeting gives a meaningful indication of how dollars are expected to turn into results'.[1] It does this by showing for each program area how dollars fund day-to-day activities, how those activities lead to outputs (the volumes of goods and services produced) and then what outcomes (impacts within society) should result. Mercer has developed what he calls 'Cascade Performance Budgeting' (May 2003), which consists of four principal steps:

- reformatting the budget along the lines of department's strategic plan;
- illustrating through tables and diagrams the connections between budgets and strategic goals;
- linking day-to-day activities to this chain of performance budgets; and,
- displaying the full costs of these activities in a manner that facilitates the calculation of the total cost of achieving goals.

Even though it was first developed in the small (130,000 people) California city of Sunnyvale (where Mercer was Councillor and Mayor), it is claimed that 'the general structure and methodology for developing a Cascade™ Performance Budget is similar for all government applications'.[2] **Exhibit 6** provides a conceptual overview of the components of CPB and **Exhibit 7** provides an actual example of downward reporting on performance for a particular program.

There is no disputing the sophistication of the CPB approach — with its vertical and horizontal linkages to capture information about different dimensions of programs and the interactions among programs. In addition to the conceptual and analytical challenges of applying the approach, there are the costs of doing so. To produce the comprehensive, valid, reliable, comparable and continuous performance data called for in the CPB model would be a massive and expensive undertaking. It would require training of program staff and an enormous amount of staff time. Since budgets are already prepared under great pressures of time and with an overriding focus of meeting government priorities and serving ministers, it is doubtful whether such a performance budget could be produced in time to guide decision-making. This raises the important point that performance measurement systems must themselves be subject to cost-effectiveness evaluation. In principle, such systems should provide 'relevant' and 'adequate' data at a 'reasonable' cost. As the quotation marks suggest, what is relevant adequate and reasonable involves a subject judgement.

There is another problematic aspect to the insistence that performance measurement be tied directly and immediately to budgetary decision-making. Doing this will make performance measurement more threatening. In a time of budgetary restraint and cutbacks, performance reporting can be seen as a 'gotcha tool' for the Treasury Board and the Auditor General. If the centre demands performance information, it will be provided, but often in a desultory and cautious manner. Partly to protect the minister, the department, their programs and their own reputations, managers will volunteer negative news reluctantly, if at all. As Douglas Hartle, a shrewd observer of the budgetary process, once wrote: "It is a strange dog that willingly carries the stick with which it is beaten."[3] In most jurisdictions, departments have been asked to absorb the costs of producing performance reports without additional resources and many probably feel that the money could be better spent directly on programs.

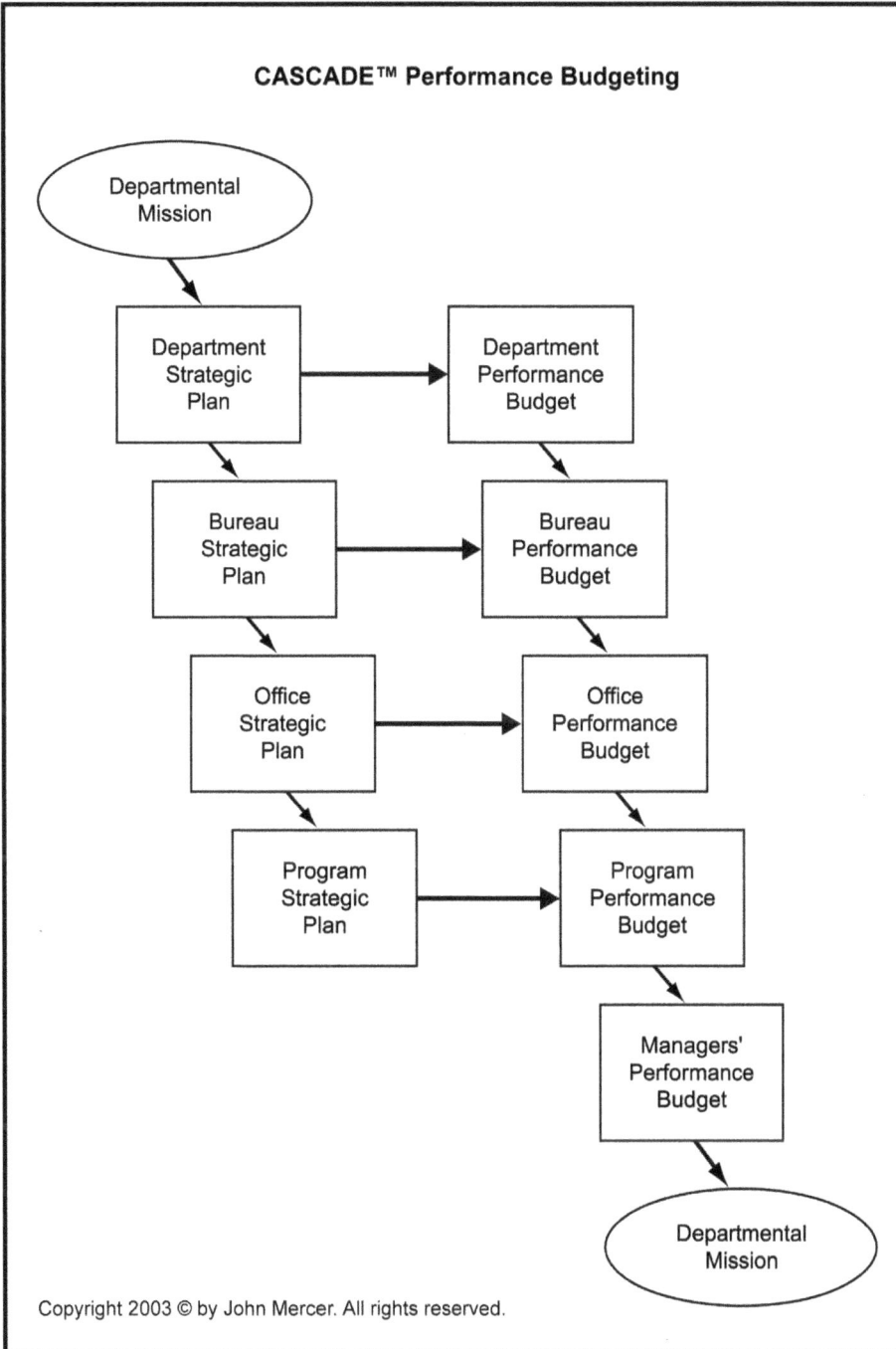

Exhibit 6

CASCADE™ Performance Budgeting

```
   ┌───────────────┐
   │ Departmental  │
   │   Mission     │
   └───────┬───────┘
           ↓
   ┌───────────┐         ┌───────────────┐
   │Department │────────→│  Department   │
   │ Strategic │         │  Performance  │
   │   Plan    │         │    Budget     │
   └─────┬─────┘         └───────┬───────┘
         ↓                       ↓
   ┌───────────┐         ┌───────────────┐
   │  Bureau   │────────→│    Bureau     │
   │ Strategic │         │  Performance  │
   │   Plan    │         │    Budget     │
   └─────┬─────┘         └───────┬───────┘
         ↓                       ↓
   ┌───────────┐         ┌───────────────┐
   │  Office   │────────→│    Office     │
   │ Strategic │         │  Performance  │
   │   Plan    │         │    Budget     │
   └─────┬─────┘         └───────┬───────┘
         ↓                       ↓
   ┌───────────┐         ┌───────────────┐
   │  Program  │────────→│   Program     │
   │ Strategic │         │  Performance  │
   │   Plan    │         │    Budget     │
   └───────────┘         └───────┬───────┘
                                 ↓
                         ┌───────────────┐
                         │   Managers'   │
                         │  Performance  │
                         │    Budget     │
                         └───────┬───────┘
                                 ↓
                         ┌───────────────┐
                         │ Departmental  │
                         │   Mission     │
                         └───────────────┘
```

Exhibit 7

Cascade™ Drill-Down Example
End Outcome to Intermediate Outcome to Outputs to Activities for FY 2005

Strategic Goal 4. The public will be protected from unsafe practices that pose serious threats to their local environment.

   • **Strategic Objective 4.1.** Local communities will be assured of safe and proper handling of dangerous toxic chemicals.

      • **Strategic Performance Goal 4.1.1.** By FY 2008, achieve a reduction of 24% from the 2002 baseline in the number of adverse incidents designated as 'serious' in the transportation and storage of Class Al and A2 toxic chemicals.

        • **FY 2005 Annual Performance Goal 4.1.1.1.** Reduce the number of serious incidents in the transport and storage of Class Al and A2 toxic chemicals by 4% from the 2004 result.

          • **Performance Indicator 4.1.1.1 — PI.A.** No more than 3 deaths caused directly by adverse incidents involving Class Al and A2 toxic chemicals.
          • **Performance Indicator 4.1.1.1 — PI.B.** No more than 28 hospitalisations required as a direct result of adverse incidents involving Class Al and A2 toxic chemicals.
          • **Performance Indicator 4.1.1.1 — PI.C.** Length of hospitalisation is no greater than 3 days in at least 80% of cases.

          <u>Hazardous Cargo Program</u>
          • **Program Measure 4.1.1.1 — PM.A.** Reduce the number of incidents of spillage in the transport of Class Al and A2 toxic chemicals by 3% from the 2004 result.
          • **Program Measure 4.1.1.1 — PM.B.** Increase the ...

          <u>Toxics Storage Safety Program</u>
          • **Program Measure 4.1.1.1 — PM.C.** Reduce the number of incidents of spills and leaks in the storage of Class Al and A2 toxic chemicals by 5% from the 2004 result.
          • **Program Measure 4.1.1.1 — PM.D.** Achieve an average satisfaction rating of at least 3.8 on a 5-point scale from Class Al and A2 licensees on their dealings with TSSP officials.

          Activities:
          • **4.1.1.1 — 3.** Conduct 4975 inspections
          • **4.1.1.1 — 4.** Complete 1985 investigations
          • **4.1.1.1 — 5.** Issue 4100 licenses

ENDNOTES

[1] John Mercer. 'Cascade Performance Budgeting: A Guide to an Effective System for Integrating Budget and Performance Information and for Linking Long-Term Goals to Day-to-Day Activities' (May 2003) p. 5.

[2] *Ibid.* p. 1.

[3] Douglas G. Hartle. 'The Role of the Auditor General of Canada.' *Canadian Tax Journal* 23, 3 (1975). p. 197.

Performance Measurement and Evaluation

Performance reports might play their most useful role in signalling to responsible decision-makers and to others the need to conduct more systematic and in-depth evaluations of policies and programs which do appear to be working very well based on the latest published performance evidence. In some ways, performance measurement represents the successor managerial approach to program evaluation which enjoyed great popularity during the 1960s and the 1970s. Evaluation promised better informed decision-making about programs based upon periodic, systematic and objective investigations into their economy, efficiency and effectiveness in serving their declared goals. Many countries, but particularly the United States, made evaluations of programs mandatory on a cyclical basis. A large community of professional evaluators developed both inside and outside of government. However, within a couple of decades, a certain amount of discouragement overcame the evaluation community based on the difficulty and expense of measuring the success of programs and the seemingly low levels of utilisation of evaluation findings by decision-makers. In addition to the analytical and financial problems, many in the evaluation community pointed to the role that politics played in limiting the impacts of the approach.

As budgets within governments became tighter from the late 1970s onwards, 'the evaluation industry' which had been growing rapidly both inside and outside of government began to decline. Rather than make evaluation mandatory on a calendar basis, governments adopted a more selective approach to the use of evaluations. Also, evaluations became less comprehensive and did not aspire to the same level of scientific validity as in the past. Performance measurement emerged in this context partly as a lower cost alternative to expensive, in-depth evaluations. Since the new approaches derive from the same disciplines and rely upon some of the same analytical techniques, professionals who were formerly evaluators became performance measurement specialists. However, most performance measures stop short of answering fundamental questions about why programs work or fail to work. At best they sound alarms that something is wrong, suggest questions about what has happened and prompt debate about what can be done to improve programs. On this basis, performance reports can support decision to undertake a more in-depth evaluation of the operations of a program. Evaluation findings can then ideally flow into the planning, budgeting and performance measurement systems.

Telling the 'Performance Story'

With more governments issuing annual 'report cards', there is the danger that politicians, public managers, interest groups, the media, and the public at large will become mesmerised by the numbers. Excellence in the public sector could become equated with scoring high results on a limited number of measures over a short period of time. To promote deeper understanding of what the numbers mean, public organisations need to be able to 'tell their stories', as departments of the Australian government do in their impressive annual reports. Storytelling should not be dismissed as merely self-serving anecdotes. Stories serve to put measures in context and to provide explanations. It is on the basis of the stories they tell and to which they listen that public managers gain a greater understanding of and assign meaning to the changing realities of program operations. Also, plausible and vivid stories are important rhetorical and persuasive devices to gain attention for issues and action on problems. The communications requirements for promoting the use of performance evidence have not received enough attention.

The communications function of a performance measurement system needs to be approached from a strategic perspective by carefully analysing such situational and design factors as objectives for communicating, the nature of the intended and unintended audiences, the role of the sender, the context in which communication is to take place, the choice of media, and the format of the message.[1] More attention should be paid to design considerations in the presentation of information. As Edward Tufte writes, "For information displays, design reasoning must correspond to scientific reasoning".[2] Ideally, design formats should document sources, demonstrate cause and effect, promote comparison, recognise the multivariate nature of problems and indicate alternative explanations. All of this sound advice is complicated in practice by the fact that performance reports in the public sector serve multiple aims and multiple audiences.

The Office of the Auditor General of Canada (OAG) has done valuable work in developing criteria of 'quality information' and 'excellence' in reporting. It must be remembered that the focus of this work is mainly on external reporting for purposes of accountability to Parliament and the public. In a 1992 report the OAG identified the following criteria for quality information for Parliament:

Relevancy   -   meaningful, complete, timely
Reliability   -   accuracy, validity and consistency
Understandability -   clear, concise and comprehensive.

All of these terms have positive connotations. Putting operational meaning into them requires judgement about the context and the audiences' needs. Also, there may need to be 'trade-offs' among the criteria (e.g., balancing comprehensiveness with timeliness). In 2002, the OAG published a report recommending a model for rating departmental reports based on five criteria:

- organisational context and strategic outcomes are clear;
- performance expectations are clear and concrete;
- key results are reported against expectations;
- reliability of performance information is supported; and
- use of performance information is demonstrated.

This format enables the leadership of an organisation to identify the challenges it is facing. Expecting all organisations to display results in the same format within the same time frame may ignore the fact that some policy and program fields represent more difficult problems. Qualitative information is as important as quantitative information in telling the 'performance story'. Measures should be restricted to factors under 'reasonable control' by the organisation and there should be an opportunity to identify uncontrollable factors. Managers should be encouraged to discuss the causal links they believe are occurring between the outputs of the program and the evidence of the outcomes to which it has contributed. The 'performance story' will never achieve the status of scientific proof, but over time it can become more credible. To encourage improvement in performance reporting, governments might consider an award recognising the best and most improved performance reports produced annually or bi-annually. This is done for the annual reports of crown corporations within the Government of Canada.

ENDNOTES

[1] James Garnett. *Communicating for Results in Government*. San Francisco: Jossey-Bass, 1994.

[2] See Edward Tufte. *Visual Explanations*. Cheshire, CT.: Graphic Press, 1997, the third of his books on presenting quantitative and qualitative information in ways to promote deeper understanding.

The Utilisation Problem

As the above discussion suggests, the ultimate worth of any performance measurement system is the use to which it is put. The functionality of the system is therefore very important. Providing relevant and reliable information to the right people at the right time is the ideal. The depressing news from the world of practice is that the utilisation of performance evidence on all levels appears to be limited. This strong statement must be immediately qualified, however. We simply do not have many good empirical studies of the actual use of performance information at different levels and for different purposes. Governments like to boast that their performance measurement systems are widely used, but ironically they rarely provide evidence to support this claim. Outside commentators have difficulty evaluating how well systems are working because of the confidentiality surrounding key relationships within the process. The fact that performance measurement serves many aims and different audiences, it is difficult to determine whether utilisation has occurred. Does utilisation consist of the direct and immediate use of performance data to guide decision-making? Or, at the other end of a continuum, does it refer to the general enlightenment function of performance information in support of social learning?

The Oregon Benchmarks program is the most ambitious program of its kind in the United States. In the early 1990s, under the leadership of a new governor, (Neal Goldschmidt) the State created a task force to draw up a state-wide strategic vision (called Oregon Shines) and then established the Oregon Progress Board to establish a set of 'benchmarks' to measure progress towards that vision. In 1991, the legislature approved 191 benchmarks, but the Progress Board kept on proposing new ones, so that the total soon reached 272 benchmarks, more than even the most dedicated public official could follow. An even greater problem was the indiscriminate lumping together of goals that were merely challenging, with those that were heroic and some that were utterly impossible — such as cutting child abuse in half within five years. The designers of the Oregon Benchmarks understood this, but they subscribed to the view that setting very difficult targets provided an incentive for people to work harder. A contrary assumption would be that unrealistic expectations would lead to frustration on the part of the public managers and worsening cynicism on the part of the public.

The lesson from Oregon is the need to balance comprehensiveness with parsimony in the creation of a performance measurement system. Also indicators must be realistic and deal with problems reasonably within the control of the agency responsible for them. Gradually, this recognition dawned on Oregon officials, and in 1996 the number of benchmarks was reduced to a more manageable ninety. In 2000, many of the benchmarks were revised so that the state actually had a chance to meet them. There were benefits from the program — apart from the goals themselves. Information not previously available was published, inter-agency communication was encouraged and some agencies were encouraged to improve their performance. At the same time that Oregon was making its promises more realistic, Florida and Minnesota were also scaling back their performance reporting systems.

Complications

Many of the complications associated with the use of performance information have been referred to earlier in this paper. Therefore, a brief analysis will be presented of four types of complications: technical, institutional, financial and political.

The conceptual and technical problems involved with valid and reliable performance measurement are numerous. Grenier sums up the problems as follows:

> Public sector performance measurement is, in effect, like putting a meter on a black box: we have little knowledge of the mechanism inside and no theory linking inputs, processes, outputs and outcomes to explain why a particular result occurred or to prescribe what management or organisational adjustments are needed to improve performance.[1]

Given the critical role played by external forces, it is often difficult to separate program impacts from surrounding events. Different aims and different audiences look to performance measurement to provide answers to different questions. There are problems of consistency and comparability of performance measures, both over time and across organisations. Lack of agreement on what constitutes success, leads to a lack of clear standards against which performance might be judged. Making relevant information available to the right people, in the most appropriate format, on a timely basis, represents an analytical and practical challenge. Performance measures are usually backward looking; they deal with the past and do not provide a clear indication of what the future holds. Finally, most performance indicators represent 'dumb data' in the sense that they do not speak for themselves, or more precisely they say different things to different people. Performance measures will always be contestable, which is appropriate because there are no simple answer to the questions that arise in the public sector.

The financial obstacles to performance measurement are probably the most obvious and therefore require less elaboration. Information is not a free resource. To produce comprehensive, valid, reliable, comparable and continuous performance data is simply too expensive for most governments and would invite criticism that they are diverting scarce funds from actual program operations. The pragmatic response of most governments has been to focus on a select number of indicators and to draw on administrative data collected on a routine basis. While this approach is understandable it entails some risks. The practice of reporting on only a few indicators exposes governments to the disease *aggregationitis*, a condition in which a great deal of relevant information goes missing through the process of aggregation. Another consequence of cost constraints may be the measurement of the measurable only, rather than of what is truly important.

For example, quantity is usually easier to measure than quality, but without quality considerations outcomes measures will be distorted. Cost considerations may also lead to a short-run concentration in measurement, since time-series data is expensive to maintain. Ideally, there should be a comparative component to any performance measurement, and this may involve additional expenses. Reductions in performance measurement efforts have involved a weighting of the costs against the benefits and the conclusion that such systems were 'not paying their own way', either in the form of programs terminated, efficiencies gained or improvements in performance.

The main institutional barriers to utilisation of performance measurement have been described or hinted at throughout this paper:

- mandates, missions and goals of public organisations tend to be vague and controversial making it difficult to agree on operational measures;
- organisations often do not collect the most appropriate data and do not have the administrative and technological capability to gather new types of information;
- existing staff may not have the appropriate knowledge and skill to gather and to analyse the relevant performance data;
- the incentive systems within public organisations may lead to resistance or lack of commitment to performance measurement;
- leadership support may be lacking because performance measurement is seen as a tedious, expensive task; and,
- the culture of the organisation does not promote and support the constructive use of performance measures.

Achieving a supportive culture of performance management is probably the most important and most difficult goal to accomplish. At present, performance measurement has negative overtones for the people who manage public programs and those who supposedly benefit from them. It is often seen primarily as a budgetary tool to eliminate or to reduce programs seen as ineffective or inefficient. Performance reporting can amount to 'steering by remote control' by central agencies and headquarters within departments. Having talked about the empowerment of employees and the relaxation of procedural controls, 'the system' has substituted boundaries for decision-making in the form of statements of performance expectations and 'policing mechanisms' to enforce them. Managers who could not be trusted to exercise their professional judgement during earlier decades when money was more plentiful, are now being granted 'freedom' (they are not completely out of 'bureaucratic prison', only moved to a 'halfway house') when the money is gone and they must also find the resources within their operating budgets to pay for a new control mechanism.

For many managers, control is currently seen in the negative terms of identifying deviations from planned performance and assigning blame for shortcomings. The public sector needs to move its practices and culture towards a more positive conception of control that emphasises organisational learning and the design of appropriate responses on the basis of informed diagnoses of how programs are progressing. This point brings us to the political 'constraints' on performance measurement.

Public programs are born and shaped through the political process. This is appropriate and desirable within a democracy. Therefore, to talk about the constraints of politics interfering with the 'rational' processes of performance measurement and performance management within the public service is to ignore or to discount the requirements for democracy, legitimacy and political support for the actions of government. Performance measurement should be seen as a means to improve the quality of the political process, not to substitute for it.

The role of political considerations in the creation and use of performance measurement systems has been noted throughout this paper. It remains here only to reinforce some of the key points. Reflecting their origins in the political process, public programs have broad and general goals intended to attract the maximum political support. Speaking in terms of precise goals and measurable targets may be risky in terms of re-election prospects. Because performance measurement serves many audiences, there can be serious disagreement over what information is important and what constitutes successful performance. In fact, performance measures seldom explain unequivocally why particular results occur. The interpretation of a particular finding and a decision on whether follow-up action is required will depend on the dynamics of a given situation. Under access-to-information laws and with a more adversarial media, the use of performance reports cannot be easily restricted to internal use. When performance reports flow into the wider political area, the focus is most likely to be on the deficiencies of performance rather than providing a balanced picture. Moreover, because members of the public derive their impressions of government performance from 'the horror stories' which are featured so prominently in the mass media, the public concludes that 'nothing works'. These are not 'problems' for which there is a 'managerial solution', rather they are 'conditions' of political life that would have to change for performance measurement to work in the idealistic way that is intended.

ENDNOTES

1   John M. Grenier, 'Positioning Performance Measurement for the Twenty-First Century' in Arie Halachmi and Geert Bouckaert (eds). *Organisational Performance and Measurement in Public Sector.* Westport, Conn: Quorum Books, 1996, pp. 11-50.

The Disappointing Record of Performance Measurement/Management (PMM)

During the 1980s and 1990s, governments embraced PMM with enthusiasm, and often there was great fanfare involved with the launch of ambitious PMM systems. Effective PMM, it was promised, would lead to better outcomes and would strengthen democracy. The 'ideal' PMM system would do the following: have clearly defined purposes; focus on outcomes (not just inputs and outputs); use a limited number of measures; use measures that are valid, reliable, comparable and controllable; produce information that is timely, relevant, meaningful, balanced, and valued by key decision-makers; be integrated with planning, budgeting and evaluation activities; and would be widely understood, supported, and embedded in the culture of the organisation. Obviously, this ideal is a destination never reached, it represents an aspirational statement of what governments were striving to accomplish with their new, often expensive, PMM systems.

After two decades of design and development, PMM systems have entered a new stage in their life cycle — they might be described as beyond the awkwardness of their teenage years, not yet having reached mature, comfortable middle age, but far enough into adulthood that it is time to take stock of where they are going in the future. At the outset, governments tended to oversell the potential of PMM systems and to downplay the complications and pitfalls involved. This may have been necessary to 'sell' the idea to a sceptical public and to overcome resistance within the public service, but the inflated claims made on behalf of the new PMM systems have contributed to a sense of disappointment about what can be accomplished through this approach.

Before analysing the difficulties involved with implementing the PMM ideal, it is necessary to acknowledge the real progress that has been made in the field over the past two decades. PMM has become an accepted and institutionalised part of how governments operate today. There is a growing commitment by politicians at all levels of government to the idea of regular and meaningful reporting on performance, both for internal management purposes and for accountability to the public. Although not without some grumbling, most public managers eventually embraced performance management, developed their knowledge and skills of performance measurement, and found money within their existing budgets to put PMM systems in place, since usually no new money was available. On the analytical front, real progress has been made in measuring dimensions of government performance previously thought to be unmeasurable.

Creative conceptualisations and increasingly sophisticated analysis have been part of this learning process. Demonstrating the linkages between inputs, outputs and outcomes remains a significant challenge in many areas (especially where horizontal policy and program initiatives are involved), but even here governments have made headway with techniques like service effort and accomplishment (SEA) reporting, data envelopment analysis (DEA) and results chains. In countries with longer experience (such as Australia and the UK), there has been evolution away from narrow bottom lines to multi-dimensional assessments, from reliance mainly on quantitative data toward the integration of qualitative information and growing efforts to bring citizen (often unfortunately labelled 'customer') perspectives into the performance management process. Although systematic, empirical studies of utilisation are largely missing, reports from government present many examples of where evidence about performance has contributed to political and managerial decision-making. In terms of external accountability, there is more information available to legislatures, interested groups and organisations within society and to the people at large.

Despite these accomplishments, some leading jurisdictions in the field have recently reduced their PMM requirements. For example, in the United States at the national level, Congress started the PMM ball rolling in 1993 when it passed the Government Performance and Results Act. This statute was intended to require departments and managers to develop measures based upon strategic plans and to integrate performance information into budgeting and managerial decision-making. Recent congressional hearings about the impact of the GPRA have heard a flurry of complaints about too many measures, poor outcomes measures, a lack of common performance measures, poor coordination of measurement across related programs, and poor linkages of measurement activities to planning, budgeting, personnel systems, and to contracts/grants to third parties delivering public programs.

At the state level in the United States, Maria Aristigueta has demonstrated how the five leading governments in the field (Florida, Minnesota, Oregon, Texas and Virginia) all were forced by costs and lack of utilisation to drastically reduce their commitment to performance measurement.[1]

Similarly, in the United Kingdom, the Blair government released a document with its last budget (review of Devolved Decision-Making, March 2004) that promised a major reduction in the requirements that hospitals, schools, and local governments regularly report on and manage on the basis of performance indicators. *Indicatoritis* involving the proliferation of reporting requirements had led to information overload, to *gamesmanship* by the bodies funded by the central government and to a widening of disparities in services when funding was directed to the 'star' performers. While not scrapping the system, the Blair government promised more selective and careful use of performance information.

The Government of Canada's approach to PMM has been more cautious and experimental than other countries. During the mid 1990s, the government began with a small number of departments volunteering to produce performance reports intended to serve both internal management and external accountability purposes. The performance information was gathered and reported along 'business lines', which were usually based on individual programs but could involve the grouping of two or more related programs serving the same objectives. Based upon these initial pilot projects, the government eventually required all departmental and non-departmental bodies to report on performance so that today over 80 entities table annual reports with Parliament. Beginning in 2000, the Government of Canada added another annual report (entitled Canada's Performance, 2000) that presents what is officially described as a whole-of-government view on results covering key areas of responsibility for the national government. Through a process of expansion and refinement, this broad social indicators report now covers seven 'enduring federal roles', 23 'horizontal areas of impact', and 256 'strategic outcomes.' The long-term ambition is to revise the horizontal areas in line with shifting government priorities to map all departmental strategic outcomes and to present expenditure information for all departments by both horizontal area and strategic outcomes. There is an immense amount of work and more than a little subjective judgment involved with defining, measuring and reporting on performance along the lines of this multi-level model.

Canada is one of the few countries in the world to combine departmental business-line reporting (DPR) with a whole-of-government, social indicators approach. Linking the two levels of analysis and reporting is proving difficult and expensive. To the best of my knowledge, no full assessment of the impact of Canada's PMM system has been conducted. However, studies from the Office of the Auditor General suggest that DPRs are not comprehensive and balanced, and integration of planning, budgeting and performance management has not been achieved to any great extent. In terms of the goal of greater external accountability, Parliament and its committees have made almost no use of the DPRs or of the social report card on the country's progress. In short, at this point, the elaborate and expensive PMM system would itself probably fail a cost effectiveness analysis.

ENDNOTES

[1] Maria Aristiguesta. *Managing for Results in State Government*. Westport, Ct. Quorum Books, 1999.

The Obstacles to PMM

Why are Canada and other countries finding it so difficult to create a relevant set of performance measures and use them as a basis for action to improve performance? The reasons are numerous, and some of the more concrete constraints are discussed below. However, on the most fundamental level, the challenge arises from the inherent difficulty of the central tasks involved. Both performance measurement and performance management represent a contemporary version of the scientific management theory that dominated management thinking many decades ago. Derived from the experiences of private firms, performance measurement and performance management were oversold as offering an objective and rational approach to overcoming the constraints of 'politics' and the bureaucratic habits of self-preservation that blocked improvements in government performance.

In practice, PMM in the public sector has more resembled performance art than scientific management. This reflects the different context of a large, complex governmental system compared to the simpler context of most individual firms. Use of measures to guide action only works well when there are clear, tangible, and uncontentious goals, when the production process for achieving those goals is well understood, and when there is relative stability within the system. In government, of course, the goals are multiple, vague, contentious and shifting. Lack of knowledge, multiple uncertainties and various kinds of risk are involved with the pursuit of such goals. Rather than being stable and relatively predictable, the governmental system changes direction and content in response to election outcomes and shifts in public opinion, often reflecting short-term, high profile events.

Measures are generally considered 'good' if they are tangible, valid, reliable, understandable, comparable, timely and economical. At the highest levels of decision making within government, few measures meet these criteria, and intuitive decision-making predominates. Intuitive decision-making occurs when facts are limited or in dispute, when values and interests are in conflict, when future consequences of action are uncertain, when there are several plausible alternatives, and when time is limited. Cabinet ministers and senior public servants operating in the intuitive mode are not likely to draw upon 'hard' measures, preferring to rely on 'softer' forms of knowledge. Intuitive thinking draws on sources of intelligence other than data and employs different kinds of knowledge, especially that derived from experience and past exercises of judgment. Such approaches to understanding and decision making do not necessarily lead to poorer results than actions driven by performance evidence. Actions are more easily deduced from measurement at lower levels of public organisations because goals are simpler and operational in character, the production processes are better understood, and there is more stability within less complicated systems.

These fundamental limitations of PMM in the public sector lead to more obvious practical constraints on the use of performance evidence to achieve improved results. For the sake of simplicity and space, these constraints will be discussed briefly under four headings: technical, financial, institutional, and political.

The technical problems involved with PMM are numerous, but significant headway has been made in measuring dimensions of performance previously thought to be unmeasurable. Despite analytical advances, it remains difficult to attribute societal outcomes to government interventions, especially when more than one program or level of government is involved. Lack of agreement on what qualifies as 'success' leads to a lack of clear standards to judge performance. Most measures represent 'dumb data' in the sense that they do not speak for themselves; or more precisely, they say different things to different people. Providing comparable performance information for the varied organisations that comprise government is difficult. Different audiences look to performance measurement to provide evidence for different kinds of action. Aggregation of data necessary to avoid information overload, leads to the loss of information and the contextual knowledge needed to support fully informed decision-making. Finally, providing complete, meaningful and actionable information to the right people in the right format, at the right time represents both an analytical and practical challenge.

The financial challenge involved with PMM is relatively straightforward. It is expensive to produce comprehensive, valid and consistent performance information. Most governments have insisted that their public services do this with no new money or even during a time of budgetary cutbacks. The pragmatic response has been to focus on a select number of indicators, often based on what the governing party has promised and/or what the public is alleged to want to know. Cost considerations often lead to reliance on routinely gathered administrative data and to a short-run focus since new and continuous data generation is expensive. Another consequence of pragmatism is to measure what is measurable about performance rather than what is truly important, such as the quality of services and the progress achieved within society.

Institutional obstacles to the practice of PMM can be numerous. Organisations may not have the administrative and technological capability to gather the relevant data. There may be a requirement for training to provide staff with the appropriate knowledge and skills. Leadership from the minister and the department or agency head may be lacking because they know that news about performance will not always be good. Negative news, it is feared, will be used by budgetary agencies to eliminate or to reduce programs seen as ineffective or inefficient. And negative news will also attract outside scrutiny and criticism.

The quantitative emphasis of performance measurement might be seen as biased against organisations that deliver less tangible services to address more complex social problems. In short, based on their mandate, leadership, administrative infrastructure, staff capabilities, and internal cultures, different public organisations will be more or less ready to rise to the challenges of performance measurement and performance management.

Political considerations, broadly defined, are central to explaining the poor record of PMM. By 'politics' I mean the need to recognise and to accommodate competing interests and values within society, a process reflected in the dynamics of cabinet and bureaucratic decision-making within government. Public organisations and public programs are born and shaped through the political process, which is appropriate in a democracy. Therefore, to talk about the constraints of politics interfering with the rational processes of performance measurement and performance management is to ignore or to discount the requirements for legitimacy and public support for the actions of government. Performance measurement should be seen as a way to improve the quality of the political process, not to substitute for it. If PMM is to strengthen democracy, more ingenious methods and greater efforts must be used to incorporate public perspectives into the process, particularly the views of those segments of society that are deemed to be the beneficiaries of policies and programs.

Reflecting their origins in the political process, public organisations and public programs have broad, rhetorical goals intended to maximise political support. This makes it difficult to devise precise measures. As presently practiced, cabinet-parliamentary government tends to be mainly adversarial, negative, and theatrical. To err may be human, but in politics it leads more to blaming than to learning. As part of the permanent election, which is the essence of parliamentary life on a daily basis, opposition parties have a stake in denigrating the performance of government. Ministers and their public service advisors seek to cover up or react defensively when scandals, failures or deficiencies in performance are exposed. In short, the current culture of parliamentary government clashes with the ideal of a PMM system, in which a balanced, constructive and learning approach is assumed. These fundamental facts of political life were not adequately recognised when PMM systems were introduced. The staunchest of proponents of such systems assumed that performance was 'out there' to be objectively discovered, measured and improved. In fact, performance is a subjective and social construct that arises out of the political process and will always involve controversy.

The analytical, financial, institutional and political obstacles described above make PMM more difficult, but not impossible. Acknowledging them should lead to more realistic expectations for two seemingly rational processes operating in the political context of a complicated, dynamic and highly diversified governmental system. During the 1980s and 1990s, most governments embraced the mantra, 'if you can't measure it, you can't manage it'. If this were indeed true, large parts, including some of the most socially important parts of government activity, would be unmanageable because what is produced is intangible and subjective, and how it is produced is uncertain. Intangibility and subjectivity are not excuses not to measure, but concrete measures may miss the most important dimensions of government interactions. The assumption that PMM systems can generate the necessary evidence to explain the causal linkages between inputs, outputs and outcomes, to serve as the basis for better management and in turn, better performance (about which everyone agrees) has proven naïve and unrealistic. Moreover, some measurement is not always better than none; and there are other types of knowledge, such as intuition derived from experience, which can provide a more reliable guide to action than the latest measures. Measurement creates the impression of science, objectivity, credibility and continuous improvement. This explains why PMM acquired such symbolic (and to a lesser extent, practical) importance within governments during the past two decades when they were facing severe financial stress and deep voter discontent. Governments oversold the promise of PMM. Recent stock taking in the leading jurisdictions has created more realistic expectations and led to a scaling back of PMM efforts. Yet governments cannot and should not abandon their efforts in the field.

Accountability Versus Performance?

Accountability has always been a central concern of both the study and the practice of public management. The concept has also been elusive and controversial. Critics have seldom been hard pressed to find fault with existing accountability arrangements and procedures. When something has gone seriously wrong within government, the tendency has been to adopt wider definitions of accountability and to add new layers of accountability requirements. An ironic consequence of the expansion of the meaning of accountability has been to create even greater confusion about who is accountable for what in government.

As I have argued elsewhere, my own preference is to restrict the use of the term accountability to situations where an authoritative relationship exists.[1] Accountability should be seen as a formal relationship governed by a process and shaped in practice by the surrounding environment and culture. The formal relationship involves a person or body assigning or negotiating with others the performance of certain responsibilities, ideally based on agreed-upon expectations and standards. Persons and bodies assigned responsibilities are obliged to answer for their performance, and it is usually assumed that they are subject to penalties for non-performance and rewards for successful performance. For accountability to be fairly enforced requires that the responsible persons or bodies be given the capacity to deliver results through some combination of authority, resources, control over events and, in general, a supportive environment. The authoritative party in the relationship also has an obligation to ensure that there has been compliance with directions and expectations. Accountability breakdowns can occur, not only because individuals and organisations fail to perform, but also because the authorising bodies lack the will and/or capacity to provide clear direction for and/or careful scrutiny of performance.

Focusing responsibility and accountability with government has become more difficult because activities and programs are increasingly interdependent and collaborative in nature. The traditional, individualistic interpretation of accountability does not fit with the growing reality of a horizontal and collective approach to problem solving. The rise of 'joined up' government (a phrase popularised by the Labour Government in the U.K.) is one of the factors pushing governments away from 'procedural' (compliance) accountability and towards 'performance' (results) accountability. In theory at least, the collection, analysis and publication of performance information will enable legislatures and the public to hold both ministers and public servants more accountable.

A number of countries — most notably New Zealand — have used the distinction between **outputs** and **outcomes** to delineate the respective responsibilities and accountabilities of ministers and public servants. Under legislation passed by the New Zealand Parliament in the late 1980s, a new public sector management model was created that made senior public servants more directly and personally accountable for the performance of their departments.[2] Ministers remained responsible for outcomes through the setting of policy goals and the allocation of resources. However, the department heads (in New Zealand, *Chief Executives*) were made accountable for the outputs (programs, services, activities, financial management, contractual arrangements, etc.). Appointed by the Cabinet on the recommendation of the State Services Commissioner for five-year terms, the Chief Executives (CEs) were also subject to annual performance appraisals and eligible for performance-based pay increases. Part of the personal contract for CEs involves the purchase by the minister of policy advice, service delivery and regulation from the department. To guide ministers and departments in their performance efforts, the Cabinet issues an annual document called Strategic Results Areas (SRAs). SRAs were part of the accountabilities set down in the performance agreements of CEs. Internal accountability of CEs to their individual ministers is achieved through the use of plans, budgets, financial reports and a series of Key Results Areas (KRAs). External accountability to Parliament is based on the tabling of plans, budgets, estimates and annual reports. Ministers appear before parliamentary committees to answer for outcomes, the financial framework and the overall operation of the department. But the CE appears on his or her own behalf to answer for the efficiency and effectiveness of the outputs of the department.

Debate continues to rage over the desirability and workability of the New Zealand model of public management. Its defenders make a series of arguments in defence of separating policy from management and making the most senior manager contractually accountable to the government and the minister:

- it clarifies the policy leadership role of ministers;
- it discourages ministers from 'meddling' in administrative matters for partisan reasons;
- it recognises that the daily running of departments is in the hands of permanent officials and they should be held accountable for the efficiency and effectiveness of the department; and,
- it recognises that the management challenges are not the same in each department and individual contracts provide a fairer basis for appraising the performance of the department head.

Critics of the N.Z. model — especially as it has worked in practice over the past decade — raise the following concerns:

- just as it is difficult to separate policy from management, similarly the separation of the respective responsibilities of ministers and department heads is equally problematic;

- success requires that they work as partners;
- by their formal nature contracts signify a lack of trust and confidence in a relationship which demands candour and mutual support;
- contracts can lead to inflexibility and over-emphasis on particular tasks that are easily identified and measured;
- holding department heads personally accountable for efficiency and sound financial management narrowly defined might be appropriate, but it would be inappropriate and unfair to hold them accountable for the effectiveness of policies and programs when ministers choose to adopt ambitious goals and fail to provide adequate resources; and,
- when something goes seriously wrong, ministers will be tempted to place the blame on senior public servants and they may counter that their department was not given the tools to do the job.

This last scenario of 'blame avoidance' is not far fetched. Under the traditional understanding of complete ministerial responsibility for all departmental activities, it is possible (and increasingly frequent) for ministers to shift blame for unwanted events to public servants. But the formal separation of responsibilities and the use of contracts will make this more of a possibility.

There are pressures on all organisations to learn faster and to manage their knowledge better. The adoption of performance measurement systems reflects this requirement. A more decentralised and flexible public service which is searching for valid and reliable performance results must strive for policy creativity and administrative innovation. However, our current understanding and approach to accountability gets in the way of policy and organisational learning. Nearly all the emphasis in terms of the practice of accountability is about preventing 'screw-ups' and pointing the finger of blame when something goes wrong. There needs to be a shift away from accountability as 'blaming' and towards an emphasis on accountability as 'learning'. Not every change made within government will be a success. Some unforeseen and unpreventable errors will occur. This needs to be better understood and more accepted. What is required is mainly a cultural shift.

Ministers cannot demand innovation and also insist on error-free government. Public servants should not be made the scapegoats for problems that arise more from poor policy design and/or inadequate resources than from managerial shortcomings. In short, 'remedial accountability', meaning the acceptance of responsibility to fix problems and to prevent their recurrence, needs to be relied upon more. And, 'punitive accountability', meaning the automatic insistence on ministerial resignations and/or the 'public hanging' of public servants, needs to be relied upon less. Achieving this cultural shift in our understanding of accountability will be difficult because of the strong adversarialism in Parliament, the sensational media coverage of political events and the public's insistence that someone should pay a significant price when untoward events occur in government.

ENDNOTES

[1] Paul G. Thomas. 'Introduction to the Section on Accountability' in B. Guy Peters and Jon Pierre (eds). *Handbook of Public Administration*. London: Sage, 2003. pp. 549-56.

[2] Jonathon Boston, John Martin, June Pallot and Paul Walks, *Public Management: The New Zealand Model*. New York: Oxford, 1996.

The Future of PMM

Up to now, governments have focused on designing and implementing measurement systems. As these systems move into a more mature phase, the emphasis must shift to how we use measurement to manage better. How can we define and operationalise various concepts and dimensions of performance to make them more amenable to meaningful measurement? How can we extract greater insight about what works, and why, from available data? How can we better communicate those insights to the multiple audiences served by the performance measurement system? How can we ensure that measurement influences policy formation and managerial behaviour, which in turn leads to improved outcomes? How do we apply the PMM approach to horizontal areas of policy-making and service delivery that transcend departmental and governmental boundaries? How do we employ PMM to improve the management and results of contracting out service delivery to third parties? Finally, how do we ensure that performance measurement is itself both cost-effective and accountable? These are the areas that governments, consultants and academics should be addressing in the future.

In the future, less emphasis should be placed on reporting data and more should be placed on allowing program managers to tell 'the performance story.' Managers have the most intimate knowledge of the context in which effective performance is being sought. They know what factors — both within and beyond their control — influence outputs and outcomes. If judgments about programs are to be well informed, and if accountability is to be fairly enforced, there must be a recognition of the contextual factors that condition performance. Allowing organisations to tell their own story involves the risk of self-congratulatory, or at least flattering, reports that lack credibility. To counter this natural tendency, the challenge function represented by Parliament and its committees would need to be strengthened. MPs would have to become more committed to understanding performance and be prepared to contribute constructively to its improvement, as opposed to always playing partisan games. More professional staff for committees would be needed.

For the future, we should see PMM as less about sophisticated conceptualisation and precise analysis and more about interaction and seeking a consensus on what should be measured, how and with what consequences. The process should be less top-down and bureaucratic. It should involve consultation with the key stakeholders and the public at large, so that the results of the PMM system have more legitimacy and support, especially among the people most directly affected by programs. This would also improve the relevance and importance of performance reports in the eyes of ministers and parliamentarians. Under this model, communications becomes a strategic activity, not simply a debate over how best to array information in order to present in the best possible picture of performance. Ideally, a reasonably informed, interested user should be able to learn about the availability of performance reports and should be able to access, understand and use reported performance information. Consistency in reporting to allow for comparison must be balanced with the need to adapt and improve performance measures. Given the multiple, potential audiences for its performance reports, information should be presented on a number of levels and should be communicated through a variety of mediums, suitable to the various intended users. None of this is easy, but a shift in focus from measurement per se to communication about performance would be a valuable first step.

Measuring outcomes will continue to be the 'Holy Grail' of performance management and the most challenging analytical task faced by program managers. Understanding the linkages among inputs, outputs, and eventual outcomes within society is obviously crucial to learning and improvements in actual performance. However, governments, Parliament and others must recognise that outcomes are problematic for accountability purposes, for such recognised technical reasons as attribution difficulties, multiple causality, and long time scales. It is inefficient and unfair to hold ministers and departments accountable for eventualities over which they have limited control. A robust performance-based approach to accountability based on measured outputs and intermediate outcomes should not be ridiculed as second-rate because the valid attribution of outcomes in society to governmental actions will remain an elusive goal.

Attribution issues will become an even greater challenge as governments are increasingly 'joined up' with one another and seek to achieve more holistic, integrated approaches to policy/program development and service delivery. Coordination of performance measurement, reporting and management across programs, departments, orders of government, and private contractors providing public services will become more important in order to avoid duplication, lack of consistency and/or gaps in coverage. Also, in the world of joined-up governments and growing requirements for horizontal management, there must be a substitution of more collective and constructive approaches to accountability for the present approaches, which are mainly individual in focus, negative in tone, and end up blocking organisational learning.

A shift to a collective and constructive approach to accountability will be more cultural than it is organisational and procedural. The political and administrative cultures of government overlap and intersect. As noted above, the political culture of cabinet-parliamentary government is mainly adversarial and theatrical, leading ministers to insist on error-free performance and causing public servants to be risk adverse. Publishing results on a regular basis, and having honest debates about shortcomings in performance can prove embarrassing and damaging to the reputations of governments. Until this external political culture changes, more balanced and forthright discussions of performance will not take place.

Learning from success *and* failure

The tendency to date has been to follow a 'best practice' approach searching for what works elsewhere. The risk of this approach is that it takes inadequate account of the particular circumstances of different organisations. We need to examine both **successful** and **unsuccessful** efforts to introduce performance measurement. **Exhibit 8** presents a listing of some of the general conditions needed to support the development of an effective performance measurement system. Although we can learn from 'leading' organisations, we also need to examine the experiences of 'not-so-successful' organisations that are trying to improve their performance measurement efforts in spite of the constraints identified throughout this paper.

Exhibit 8 — Conditions Favouring Performance Measurement

- Agreement on what constitutes performance.
- Activities involved are amenable to measurement on a quantitative or qualitative basis.
- Cause-effect relations are reasonably well understood and attribution is possible.
- Scale of operations is large enough to spread the costs of designing and operating the measurement system.
- Leadership support for the activity and the culture of the organisation supports dialogue over what the evidence is saying.

Decades of past efforts to improve public sector performance suggest that progress is more likely to be made on a gradual, incremental basis than on the basis of s single spectacular breakthrough. Consistent with the main theme of this paper, **Exhibit 9** offers 'A Bakers' Dozen Hints for Better Performance Measurement'. This is meant as a small reward for the durable reader who has persevered to the end of a long paper.

Exhibit 9 — A Bakers' Dozen Hints for Better Performance Measurement (PM)

1. Conduct a feasibility study to determine the readiness of your organisation to develop a PM system.
2. Develop an approach to PM, which fits with the mission and nature of the tasks of your organisation.
3. Consult the relevant stakeholders before adopting measures or indicators for your organisation and its programmes.
4. Link measurement activities to strategic/business plans.
5. Set forth as clearly as possible performance expectations and compare to actual results.
6. Strive for balance in your PM system between: comprehensiveness vs. relevance/simplicity; financial vs. non-financial, short-term vs. longer-term; control vs. learning, outputs and outcomes; quality from an internal, professional perspective with quality from an external, user perspective.
7. Promote a culture of performance management within your organisations. Create incentives or remove disincentives for the use of performance measure.
8. Encourage the development of causal models of programmes which link outputs to desired outcomes.
9. Ensure fairness in the use of performance data to appraise the performance of organisations and individuals. Allow for the recognition of factors beyond their control.
10. Approach the task of communicating about performance in a strategic fashion by paying attention to the needs of different audiences.
11. Take a pragmatic approach: use pilot projects in areas more amenable to measurement, make use of existing data sources, acknowledge the limits of existing data, but do not wait for the 'best' data to become available and review the cost-effectiveness of your system periodically.
12. Consider benchmarking your performance to that of superior comparable organisations and share knowledge with other organisations.
13. Recognise the limits of measures. Don't be mesmerised by the numbers. Ensure the continued relevance of your measures. Avoid doing the wrong things well, based on your PM system.

Conclusions

The above discussion was not meant to debunk performance measurement or to produce a sense of futility that the approach will contribute nothing of value to government. Rather, the purpose was to explain why performance measurement systems have delivered less than was hoped for. The explanation has been wide ranging, drawing attention to a number of factors but the main emphasis has been on the fact that performance measurement is a 'rational' management technique operating in a political context where other types of rationality often prevail. The most appropriate stance to adopt on performance measurement is realism about its potential and its problems. This will involve steering a reflective and practical, middle course between naïve faith in rational techniques and the cynical use of performance measurement for purely symbolic purposes. It is my impression that most public servants strive to find this difficult, middle ground between commitment and cynicism. They are not opposed to measuring performance; they are realistic about the possibilities of doing so and of using the findings to shape policy and management decisions.

Performance measurement is here to stay. Interested members of the public are becoming accustomed to the regular appearance of performance reports in many policy fields. There is a growing commitment by politicians at all levels of government to the idea of regular and meaningful reporting on performance. Not only have most public servants embraced the notion of performance management; they have developed their knowledge and skills of performance measurement. Despite periods of budgetary restraint, public managers have found ways to finance performance measurement systems. Real progress has been made in measuring dimensions thought to be un-measurable. Demonstrating the linkage between activities and outcomes remains a serious theoretical and analytical challenge, but even here governments have made headway with techniques like 'results chains', data envelopment analysis, adjusted performance measures and Service Effort and Accomplishment Reporting. In countries with longer experiences in performance measurement (such as Australia and the United Kingdom) there has been an evolution away from narrow bottom lines to multi-dimensional assessments, from reliance mainly on quantitative information toward the integration of qualitative information and from single perspectives to multiple perspectives on performance. Reports from governments offer many examples of where performance measurement has seemingly contributed to improved performance. In terms of external accountability, there is more information available to legislatures and the public. In summary, progress has been made. If there is still a sense of disappointment, it arises partly from the inflated claims made on behalf of performance measurement schemes when they were launched.

Developing a culture of performance within the public services of Anglo-American countries will require shared leadership and a more systematic approach to cultural change than has been followed to date. Launched in the midst of downsizing, there was always the suspicion that performance measurement was mainly a budgetary tool to chop down overgrown departments and programs. At a time when there is a lot of rhetoric about reducing red tape and procedural controls in order to let managers manage, many public servants are suspicious that 'the centre' does not really trust them and continues to practice control by means such as performance measurement and reporting. Recent scandals have lead to the reimposition of many prior controls, so the overall level of internal regulation has actually increased.

For the future, a more focused approach to measurement and reporting should be used to reduce the burden on organisations and managers. The more selective approach should concentrate on information that is meaningful to managers and has the potential to support decision making and action. A more consultative and shared leadership approach should be developed as a basis for deciding what is measured, how and with what consequences. Finally, there is also the need to increase trust in reporting relationships and to create incentives for program managers to deliver comprehensive, balanced and credible news about performance. All of this will contribute to the emergence of a stronger performance culture, which ultimately is more important than the present blizzard of paper and e-files.

Selected Bibliography on Performance Measurement and Accountability

Even a selected list of sources is lengthy because so many governments are pursuing results-oriented approaches and the secondary literature on these efforts is voluminous and constantly growing. To make the bibliography easier to use, an asterisk (*) has been used to designate better sources to broaden your knowledge and deepen your understanding of the issues involved with performance measurement and reporting.

Aristigueta, Maria P. *Managing For Results in State Government*. Westport, Ct, Quorum Books, 1999.

Atkinson, Anthony A., John H. Waterhouse and Robert B. Wells. 'A Stakeholder Approach to Strategic Performance Measurement.' *Sloan Management Review* 38, 3 (Spring 1997): 25-38.

Behn, Robert D. 'The Psychological Barriers to Performance Management: Or why isn't everyone jumping on the performance management bandwagon?' *Public Performance & Management Review* 26, 1 (September 2002): 5-25.

___. *Different Purposes Require Different Measures*. (Paper presented to the Association for Public Policy Analysis and Management, Seattle, November 2-4, 2000).

Boyne, G., J. Gould-Williams, J. Law and R. Walker. 'Plans, Performance Information and Accountability: The case of best value.' *Public Administration* 80, 4 (Winter 2002): 691-710.

British Columbia, Office of the Auditor General and Deputy Ministers Council. *Enhancing Accountability for Performance: A framework and an implementation plan*. Office of the Auditor General, Victoria, 1996.

Canadian Comprehensive Auditing Foundation. *Reporting Principles: Taking public performance reporting to a new level*. CCAF-FCVI Inc., Ottawa, 2002.

Dittenhofer, Mort. 'Performance Auditing in Governments.' *Managerial Accounting Journal,* 16, 8 (2001): 138-142.

Edenius, Matt and Hans Hasselbladh. 'The Balanced Scorecard as Intellectual Technology.' *Organisation*, 9, 2 (2002): 249-73.

Feller, Irwin. 'Performance Measurement Redux.' *The American Journal of Evaluation*, 23, 4 (Winter 2002): 435-52.

Garnett, James. *Communicating for Results in Government*. Jossey Bass, San Francisco, 1994.

Gormley, William T. and David L. Weemer. *Organisational Report Cards*. Harvard University Press, Cambridge, 1999.

Halachmi, Arie and Geert Bouchaert (eds). *Organisational Performance and Measurement in the Public Sector*. Quorum Books, Westport Ct, 1996.

Hartle, Douglas G. 'The Role of the Auditor General of Canada.' *Canadian Tax Journal* 23, 3 (1975). p. 197.

Harvard University, Kennedy School of Government, *Executive Session on Performance Management*, 2001 [www.ksg.harvard.edu/visions/performance_management]

Hall, Christine and Stephen J. Rimmer. 'Performance Monitoring and Public Sector Contracting.' *Australian Journal of Public Administration,* 53: 4 (December 1994): 453-61.

Heinrich, Carolyn I. 'Outcomes-Based Performance Management in the Public Sector: Implications for government accountability and effectiveness.' *Public Administration Review,* 62, 6 (November-December 2002):712-25.

Helgason, Sigurdur. *Toward Performance-Based Accountability*. Organisation for Economic Co-operation and Development, Paris, 1997.

___. and Paul Coates, 'Citizen Participation: Legitimising performance measurement as a decision tool.' *Government Finance Review,* (April 2002): 8-10.

Irwin, Tim. 'An Analysis of New Zealand's New System of Public Sector Reform.' *Performance Management in Government*. Organisation for Economic Co-operation and Development, Paris, 1996.

Jackson, Audrey and Irvine Lapsley. 'The Diffusion of Accounting Practices in the New 'Managerial' Public Sector.' *The International Journal of Public Sector Management,* 16, 5 (2003): 359-72.

Jackson, Peter M. *Measures for Success in the Public Sector*. The Public Finance Foundation, London, 1995.

Kerr, Deborah L. 'Managing Rosie the Riveter: The work between strategic planning and performance measurement.' *Public Productivity and Management Review* 17, 3 (Spring 1994): 215-21.

Kravchuk, Roberts and Ronald W. Shack. 'Designing Effective Performance Measurement Systems Under the Government Performance Results Act of 1993.' *Public Administration Review,* 56, 4 (July/August 1996): 348-58.

Leeuw, Frans L. 'Performance Auditing, New Public Management and Performance Improvement: Questions and answers.' *Accounting, Auditing & Accountability Journal,* 9, 2 (1996): 92-102.

Magd, Hesham and Adrienne Curry. 'Benchmarking: achieving best value in public organisations.' *Benchmarking: An International Journal,* 10, 3 (2003): 261-86.

Mayne, John and Eduardo Zapico-Goni, (eds). *Monitoring Performance in the Public Sector: Future directions from international experience.* Transaction, New Brunswick, NJ, 1997.

McLaughlin, John A. and Gretchen B. Jordan. 'Logic Models: A tool for telling your program's performance story.' *Evaluation and Program Planning,* 22, 1 (Spring 1999): 65-72.

Mercer, John. *Cascade Performance Budgeting: A guide to an effective system for integrating budget and performance information and for linking long-term goals to day-to-day activities.*(May 2003). [http://www.John-Mercer.com/library/cascade_pb.pdf]

Morley, Elaine, Scott P. Bryant and Harry P. Hatry. *Comparative Performance Measurement.* Urban Institute Press, Washington, DC, 2001.

National Partnership for Reinventing Government. *Balancing Measures: Best practices in performance management.* (August 1999). [http://govinfo.library.unt.edu/npr/library/papers/bkgrd/babmeasure.html]

Office of the Auditor General of Canada. 'Modernising Accountability in the Public Sector.' *Annual Report, 2002* [Chapter 9]. Ottawa, December 2002.

Office of the Auditor General of Canada. 'A Model for Rating Departmental Performance Reports'. *Annual Report, 2002* [Chapter 6]. Ottawa, April 2002.

Office of the Auditor General of Canada. 'Involving Others in Governing: Accountability at risk.' *Annual Report, 1999* [Chapter 23]. Ottawa, November 1999.

OECD, PUMA, *Managing Accountability in Intergovernmental Partnerships.* Organisation for Economic Development, Paris, 1999). [http://www.oecd.org/puma]

Paton, Rob. *Managing and Measuring Social Enterprises.* Sage, London, 2003.

Public Performance and Management Review—all issues of this journal, but especially the following theme issues:

- 'Symposium on Performance Assessment in the United Kingdom', Vol. 26, 3 (March 2003).
- 'Symposium: Performance Measurement and Managerial Thinking' 25, 4 (June 2002).
- 'Implementing Performance Government' 23, 3 (March 2000).
- 'Emerging Issues in Public Performance' 22, 3 (March 1999).

Roberts, Nancy. 'The Synoptic Model of Strategic Planning and the GPRA'. *Public Productivity and Management Review* 23, 3 (March 2000). pp. 297-311.

Rubenstein, Ross, Amy Ellen Schwartz and Leanna Steifel. 'Better Than Raw: A guide to measuring organisational performance with adjusted performance measures'. *Public Administration Review,* 63, 5(September/October 2003): 607-14.

Saskatchewan Finance, Performance Management Branch, *Accountability Framework, Planning Guidelines,* Regina, 2003.

Scales, Bill. 'Performance Monitoring of Public Service in Australia.' *Australian Journal of Public Administration,* 56, 1 (March 1997): 100-109.

Shane, Bryan. 'Performance Measurement System: A leadership driven methodology'. *Optimum,* 33, 3 (September 2003).

Smith, Peter (ed.). *Measuring Outcomes in the Public Sector.* Frances & Taylor, London, 1996.

Sorber, Bram. 'Performance Measurement in the Central Government Departments of the Netherlands.' *Public Productivity and Management Review,* 17, 1 (Fall 1993): 34-42.

Sun, Peter Yeh-Tong and John L. Scott. 'Towards Better Qualitative Measurement in Organisations'. *The Learning Organisation,* 10, 5 (2003): 258-71.

Thomas, Paul G. 'The Politics of Performance Measurement.' *Public Sector Management,* 8, 2 (1997): 17-19.

Thomas, Paul G. 'Introduction to the Section on Accountability' in B. Guy Peters and Jon Pierre (eds). *Handbook of Public Administration.* Sage London, 2003: 549-56.

Thomas, Paul G. 'The Changing Nature of Accountability' in B. Guy Peters and Donald Savoie (eds). *Taking Stock: Assessing public sector reforms.* McGill-Queen's University Press, Montreal, 1998: 348-93.

Treasury Board of Canada, *Canada's Performance 2002, Annual Report to Parliament.* Ottawa, 2002.

Treasury Board of Canada Secretariat. *Canadian Performance Measurement Initiatives.* Ottawa, 2000.

United Kingdom, National Audit Office, Report by the Comptroller and Auditor General. *Good Practice in Performance in Executive Agencies and Non-Departmental Public Bodies.* Stationery Office, London, March 2000. [http://www.nao.org.uk/publications/nao_reports/9900272.pdf]

United Kingdom, H.M. Treasury, Cabinet Office, National Audit Office, Audit Commission, Office for National Statistics. *Choosing the Right Fabric: A*

Framework for Performance Information. Stationery Office, London, 2000.

Walters, Jonathon. *Measuring Up*. Governing Books, Washington DC, 1998.

Zeppau, Mary and Tatiana Sotuakou. 'The 'STAIR' Model for Managing and Measuring Performance in the Post-modern Era'. *The International Journal of Public Sector Management*, 16, 4 (2003): 320-32.

www.ingramcontent.com/pod-product-compliance
Lightning Source LLC
Chambersburg PA
CBHW061241270326
41927CB00035B/3469